AT THE CORNER OF DESTINY AND INGENUITY

PAUL OWHADI

At the Corner of DESTINY and INGENUITY

LESSONS FROM
AN ENTREPRENEUR'S
IMPROBABLE LIFE

Forbes | Books

Published by Forbes Books, Charleston, South Carolina.
An imprint of Advantage Media Group.

Printed in the United States of America.

10 9 8 7 6 5 4 3 2 1

ISBN: 979-8-88750-213-7 (Hardcover)
ISBN: 979-8-88750-214-4 (eBook)

Library of Congress Control Number: 2024903374

Book design by Megan Elger.

To my devoted and amazing wife, Susan.

To my great children, Michelle, Jennifer, and Christopher.

To my mentor, Sheldon L. Pollack.

CONTENTS

INTRODUCTION

Live life as if everything is rigged in your favor.

—RUMI

We all look for teachers as we journey through our lives. We look for meaning in the lessons from our hardships, peak moments, and successes and failures. We hopefully take the lessons to heart and then carry them with us. First, the lessons may be heavy. But the reward for learning them is a lightening of the burden.

I am a venture capitalist, a real estate developer, and a first-generation American—and in his own way, my grandfather was a developer of sorts in Iran. He was certainly one of my teachers. He would take me to a bazaar-like area, where the shops were very tight, one next to the other. A plethora of colors, noises, and scents overwhelmed the senses. Aga, what I called my grandfather (a more formal term—he did not take too kindly to the sentimental "Papa"), would bring me with him as he walked through the narrow passages, stalls, and shops on either side of us. He pointed at the various stalls and small businesses: "I own these stalls and shops. That man and his wife there are my tenants." Then he would say hello to every single tenant, stopping to ask after their children, their elderly parents, or their business, his face revealing the deepest interest. This behavior was very special in Persian culture.

In Iran, there is the concept of *taarof.* We do not have a corresponding word in English. *Taarof* is, in essence, a ritual politeness—a way to show deference to others, an elegant kindness that places politeness and etiquette above other things. For example, it is more important to be polite than to have your own comfort.

So, with *taarof,* each of my grandfather's tenants would say, "Please take some fruit." The next might say, "Take some fabric," or "Bring these dates to your family"; take this, take that. Each stall or shop offered him something. They were flattered that the owner was there taking an interest in how they were doing. Did my grandfather need any of these things? No, but he would show extreme gratitude for each gift. I would walk beside Aga, carrying a sack. It was my job to take each offering with a humble, appreciative expression and put it in the bag, which I then carried all the way back to his beautiful house with its fig trees and distinct arched windows. By the time we would arrive there, between the heat and my now-heavy sack, I would be exhausted and miserable, and my shoulder would hurt from lugging the gifts home.

Then he would say, "Come into my office." He had an elegant office at his house. This was like being invited into the inner sanctum. There he had a large Honduras-mahogany box, and he would open it and take out some money.

Solemnly, he would press the reward into my palm, just a few coins, but to me a fortune. "You earned this. Remember you worked hard. And if you work hard and do an excellent job, you should receive compensation."

When he passed away, all of my siblings, all of his children, they asked for this, for that, mementos or belongings that had meaning to them or perhaps some value. But I asked for that box, which I have sitting on the mantle of the fireplace in one of my homes. When I touch that box, if I close my eyes, it takes me exactly to that place and time. I was hot, I was miserable, and my feet were dusty. I often wondered why I would always go with this old man who made me carry such a heavy thing. But when he sat there and rewarded me with a compensation for the hard work of the day and offered me cool lemonade, my *perception* changed. My money in my pocket, my thirst quenched, and my misery replaced with pride.

The sack was emptied—physically. But figuratively, it held lessons of humility, hard work, pride, appreciation, and gratitude.

I carried that sack of lessons with me—until those lessons were no longer heavy. In fact, I could then give those lessons away to others and, in turn, add new ones.

What are the things you carry?

"I know I can, and I will": This is perhaps the first of all lessons I carried. I've tried to teach self-belief and confidence to my own children. Those very words—"I know I can, and I will"—are the words my grandchildren repeat back to me. Like many first-generation immigrants, my story has more than its share of hardship and adventure. Like all parents and grandparents, I want to impart the lessons of life and business onto the next generation—without so much of the hardship. My sack carried the heavy weight, for example, of being sent thousands of miles away to a boarding school when I was just four years old. Alone and forced to carry that particular sack—until it was no longer heavy and became light and became a part of me.

My life has been an improbable journey that has taken me from Shiraz, Iran, to England, and finally to the shores of the United

States—both the coasts. It has taken me from a first-generation immigrant with a belief in my own destiny to a very successful career. The path my life took brought me to most of the countries in the world and opened universes of wonder.

I've achieved successes I could not have imagined as a child. I could not have known my future would eventually be eight thousand miles away. The United States has afforded me opportunities. But it was my life journey and what I learned along the way that allowed me to both grab those opportunities and distill them down to essential lessons.

I have had the privilege of running whole cities—and building many properties. In 1975, I was appointed the city manager in York Town, Indiana. At that time, I was the youngest city manager in the state. From there I served as the city manager and the chief executive officer of several other cities throughout the country. I was passionate about caring for cities and the people in them—revitalizing them and bringing out what made those places vibrant. I also found passion in large building projects and being able to step back and know I was a part of creating something lasting, a legacy.

I eventually entered the field of real estate development. Over time, my interests expanded until today, when I am the key principal, chairman of the board, and/or the managing general partner of over forty active companies specializing in everything from single- and multifamily residential development including subdivisions; investment in commercial, residential, and industrial real estate properties; real estate development/joint ventures with various institutional organizations; and medical/psychological services through California Psychological Institute, serving as many children's needs as possible. Of course, this is a mouthful, but it merely means I have explored all the areas of my business passions. (And I am not done yet!)

But my story all started with a small boy—not even four years old—sent off to a French boarding school far from home. From there to where I am now, I learned that home is actually something you carry with you. It is your core center. Thus, within me are the lessons I've learned from the important figures in my life—as well as my own experiences. It feels as if I traveled the world to attain my knowledge. When I was younger, I did not always *see* what I learned and how the difficult times or triumphs were training my mind and spirit to do exceptional things. But with time and thought, I had many "aha" moments.

I learned that *perception* is reality. I learned to accept people from all different backgrounds and to treat everyone with respect. My grandfather instilled a work ethic in me that led to entrepreneurship. The priests who taught at my boarding school gifted me with the values of self-reliance and discipline and a healthy dose of tough love. My father and mother also offered love—as well as a push from the place of my birth to cultures and countries far away, places that afforded freedom we could not have in Iran. My business triumphs and setbacks—and how I overcame them and then surpassed my past achievements—are a part of what tested my mettle.

Throughout it all, though, it was about perception. That if I believe I can do it, I can. My experiences have powerfully taught me self-belief, inner-strength, courage, pluck, and more. While this book is a memoir of a life of many twists and turns, it is also meant to invite you, the reader, into my own journey and to learn with me these life lessons. By the end of this book, we will stand together at a corner—that of Destiny and Ingenuity. Those two things, perhaps more than anything else, have brought me to where I am today.

But first, we must begin in a faraway place. To the first lessons I carried and my first brush with destiny.

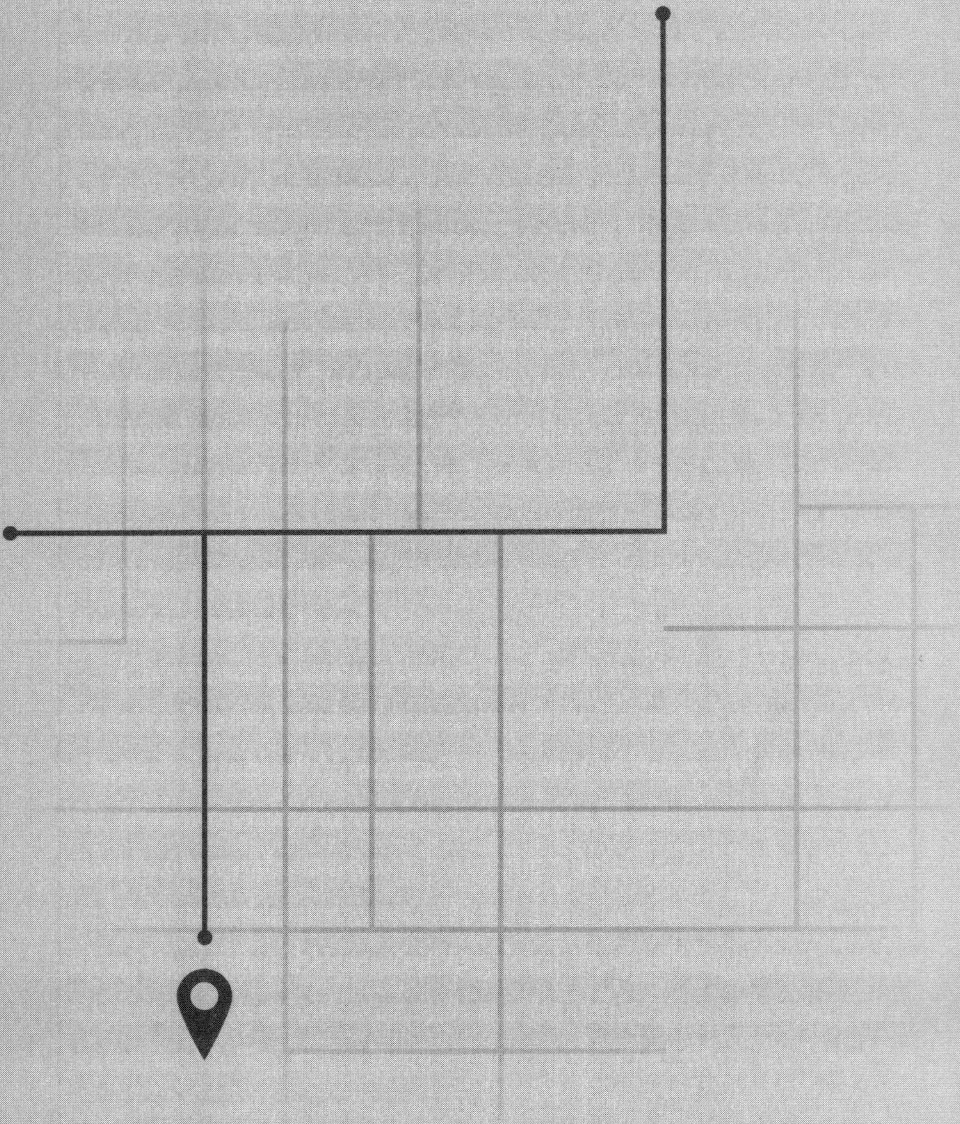

CHAPTER ONE

The Perception of Home

You don't have a home until you leave it and then, when you have left it, you never can go back.

—JAMES BALDWIN, GIOVANNI'S ROOM

We are all time travelers, able to be both where we are in the moment and somewhere in our thoughts connecting to another time, another place, to the ghosts of our past and the reality of the now. We are all on a journey, me included. And all journeys start somewhere.

The welcoming gate of the city of Shiraz, Iran, invites entry to a world of ancient buildings where you can hear the whispers of countless others who traveled those same footpaths and stones beneath your feet through the ages. Shiraz has long been considered the cultural jewel of Iran. For over a thousand years, it has been a trade center. Shiraz has also birthed thinkers and poets, such as Saadi and Hafez, who were born in the 1200s and 1300s, respectively.

Last night, from the cypress branch, the nightingale sang,
In Old Persian tones, the lesson of spiritual stations.
—HAFEZ

A famed "Pink Mosque," over 150 years old, casts a pale mauve and colorful light through its pristine stained glass as the sun rises. Shiraz is also a place of flowers, gardens, and fruit trees—and very good wine.

Shiraz is also only about thirty-five miles from the awe-inspiring ruins of the great city of Persepolis. A World Heritage Site, Persepolis dates to about 518 BC and was founded by Darius I. An architectural marvel, the palace was meant to copy Mesopotamian models. Bas reliefs and carvings depict those who came to honor the king of kings.

The sky above Shiraz, especially in summer, is a cloudless blue and so bright that it hurts your eyes. The scent of jasmine permeates the air, and *kunar* trees and green plains nestle at the foot of the Zagros Mountains, rocky giants with peaks hinting of snow.

If you listen as you wander on the path of pilgrims, you can hear the rock pigeons cooing, their wingbeats sounding in the air. And here, in this wondrous place, is where I was born, but it is not *home.* That sounds so strange, but I remember being a little boy and knowing that my future was far, far away, in the United States. I was convinced of this—and to this day I am not sure why. Could I, as a time traveler, see my future?

I was born in a British hospital in Shiraz. My parents were bicultural and exposed us beyond the boundaries and the limits of the city and place of my birth. My father, a serious, honorable man, wanted to expose me to multiple cultures. He wanted me to speak multiple languages and to see what was beyond Shiraz and beyond Iran. Like many fathers, he had dreams for who I would become, and he envisioned I might one day be a diplomat.

He was a man of few words, but those he did speak were powerful. For example, my parents classified themselves as Muslims, but they really didn't practice faithfully. They did so in the land of the shah, for the general public, for the view from outside our home looking in. But my father always said that there was no need for a middleman between me and my God.

That philosophy is one that I and my siblings all follow—and one I have passed along to my own children.

However, at almost four years old, none of this was on my mind. I was more concerned with my toys and the *ranginak* treats being made in the kitchen. But a bit before I fully turned four, I was put on a plane and sent to a French boarding school far away. In this ascetic school, priests from Switzerland, Italy, France, and Armenia tended to us. The students were from all over, so it was an instant immersion into multiple languages and cultures. There I grew up in a Catholic environment, attending daily masses on hard wooden pews under the eyes of stern priests.

I remember my first flight with my mother from the only world I knew, a verdant valley in Iran, my family, my friends, and all that was familiar, to this school, where I did not even speak the language, where I knew not one soul. I have traveled countless flights since then, have been on many adventures—including deep inside the Amazon—but I was crying and distraught on that first flight. I had a red helium balloon tied by a string to my wrist, and they had stuffed my pockets with candies, including *gaz*, a famously sweet Persian pistachio and nougat treat, all in an attempt to soothe me. The uniformed stewardess, in the formal blue skirt and blazer of flight attendants at that time, took me to the cockpit. The pilot and stewardess fussed over me and made me an honorary copilot and pinned a little set of gold wings to my jacket.

My mother was equally distraught—perhaps more so because she understood what this separation meant, how long it would truly be. When we are children, we have so little concept of time. Then, when we grow old, we realize how fast time goes by. Though I had been told I would be at the boarding school until the end of the term, I had no idea how distant that would feel, how long time would stretch for a homesick boy.

We landed and a waiting driver and car took us to the school, my face pressed against the window on my side of the back seat, taking in this completely unfamiliar place. The waiting room of my school was lined with tall, built-in, dark-wood bookshelves filled with classic texts and religious works, all aligned perfectly, their spines like sentinels. A grandfather clock stood against the far wall, its brass pendulum ticking, going back and forth, back and forth. To me, it was an ominous sound, as if my fate was being counted down. To this day, I have never allowed a grandfather clock in any of my homes.

After about ten minutes of agonizing waiting, a Swiss priest, the tall, thin, and bearded Mon Père Zuick, walked in. Even his carriage was self-contained, elegant. He gave my crying mother a moment or two to say goodbye. I clutched her, feeling her tears land on my own cheeks. Then he matter-of-factly held my hand and escorted me up to the second floor, our footsteps echoing in the stairwell. He showed me the dormitory. There were many beds lined up like the old French *Madeline* books. Only no Miss Clavel. This was a boys' world.

Number 68: that was my assigned bed. Funny how we can remember such things years later. I soon discovered that the boarding school allowed no music; in fact, absolutely *nothing* was allowed, including no conversation during lunch or dinner. If you opened your mouth, you would be punished. To our impassive Jesuit priests, silence was golden—and demanded.

It felt positively Dickensian.

But what seemed cold or lonely at first, I grew to love in my own way. Part of who I am now and why I'm here at my special corner of Destiny and Ingenuity is because of the self-reliance, integrity, and discipline I learned in that school.

We are what we repeatedly do.
Excellence, then, is not an act, but a habit.
—ARISTOTLE

The first three weeks, though, were full of hardship. I needed to learn my way among my schoolmates, boys from all over the world. I was the "new" student, and they did not make it easy for me. One time, I was beaten up badly in a schoolyard scrap. I approached Mon Père Zuick, blood gushing from my nose. He looked down at me with an imperious gaze. Then he calmly asked, "What do you want me to do about it?"

I was faced with a choice: to spend the next years of my life miserable and afraid or learn to fight back. We all know adults who shrink back when they encounter an obstacle. Then there are those of us who barrel through them, over them, around them—anything to overcome them. There I was, a four-year-old boy not even wearing long pants yet, finding the bravery inside. That is *power*. It is an internal power—not a power you lord over someone else. I could hardly have had real power over anyone else at that age. This power is what you are made of, your backbone, your heart.

I was accepted by my peers shortly after, and I learned to find my team, the boys who would truly have my back, even as children. Another lesson I filed away: *You must have the right people around you.*

One of the reasons I was accepted was my cleverness. I was skilled at making slingshots and bows and arrows. I would take the cap of the toothpaste, and I would put it on a piece of a small branch, and that became my arrow. Then I would fashion my bow. Soon, the other boys knew I was quite capable in the "important" stuff in the secret life of boys—such as defending ourselves—and they clamored for me to make bows for them too. Before I knew it, I became popular, and because of that, I gained many friends. Nobody ever touched me again.

Soon, I was thriving. I grew used to the starkness of our lives—and the ways in which we found friendships within that stone building with the morning and evening bells tolling. School was not "home," but it was a place for now. The rituals and routines became a part of me. (I still cannot "sleep in.")

Though I was able to transform my experience, I still was self-contained. We all were. Certainly, when you must eat in silence, there is no opportunity to ask others for advice. I learned that although you have the ability to get help from others, if you are not able to stand on your own feet, you are finished. There are times in life—there will always be times—that you have to make a decision, and no one else can decide for you. I developed self-confidence and faith in my own abilities. This has been one of the major keys to my success. I can speak in front of thousands of people and not have butterflies in my stomach. I can make huge decisions involving millions of dollars and impacting many people and not have any doubt. Once I make a decision, I move forward—there is little point in glancing backward other than to analyze the lessons learned, so, if it doesn't work out, you don't make the same mistake again.

I may have gotten a bloody nose when I first arrived, but Mon Père Zuick knew what I needed to do to survive and thrive in that school I came to grudgingly love. He did me a favor. Though I must confess, when I became a parent, no matter where I was in the world, I always called my children to say good night, and they never went to any boarding school. They are all wonderfully independent and smart, and I am glad they were able to learn from my experiences—and not have to get a bloody nose themselves!

Our reality is our perception. Over and over again, life has proved this very basic fact. My perception was I was brave and capable and clever. Maybe I was more frightened than I am depicting on these pages in the way our memories play subtle tricks on us. But my *perception* was that I had inner strength. So that became my reality.

My boarding school was a temporary home. Like much in life, even the difficult things, I got used to it. It was like jumping into the waters of a very cold lake in the mountains. At first, you might yelp and shiver and complain. But soon, you get used to the elements, and the water does not seem so cold. It's refreshing even.

I used to write sad letters to my parents. Mon Père Arsone would tell me that they would mail them for me, but instead, the priests would read my letters and rip them up. They never sent my words of homesickness, complaints about the food, and my longing for my mother's touch. Now, I, honestly, am glad because if my mother and father had received any of those letters, perhaps they would have brought me right back to Shiraz, and I would have missed the opportunity to discover so much about my young character.

We would rise at five o'clock, make our beds, go to Mass, recite our prayers, and memorize our Psalms. We ate breakfast in silence and then attended classes all day. Our sole entertainment was the nightly stories Mon Père Arsone, the Armenian priest, would read to us at bedtime (hence, when I learned French, it might have been with an Armenian accent!). They were usually religious stories inspiring us to be as good and brave, faithful and true as the hero in the story. We all saw ourselves as David with his slingshot or Daniel in the lion's den. We were Jonas in the belly of the whale or Noah building the great ark. The school had a projector, and on Saturdays, they would show us religious movies—and if we were lucky, a race car movie after (I never outgrew my love for race cars, and back then the famous drivers were my heroes). The only time we saw girls was on Sundays when we went to church, sat on hard wooden pews, and giggled like little fools at the sight of them.

This was our world. And I adapted to it. And then I thrived in it.

I will not say we were forced to eat gruel as in the Dickens classic *Oliver Twist.* However, we *were* forced to consume boiled spinach very frequently. In addition to not being allowed to speak during the meals, we were obligated to clean our plates regardless of what was being served. I always pretended to eat the terrible boiled spinach by dropping a chunk at the time between my legs into a napkin. I then would shove the napkin in my pocket, and at recess, I would discard the boiled spinach gradually and methodically through the holes in my shorts' pockets directly on the grounds to hide the evidence. I was like the character of Andy Dufresne in *The Shawshank Redemption*, spreading his pebbles over the prison yard. I often was hungry and craved a decent meal.

One late afternoon, I was passing by the special dining room belonging to the Mon Pères, and the smell of good food made me do the unthinkable. I recruited a buddy of mine to fetch a pillowcase from the dormitory, and then we trespassed into the forbidden zone. The table was set so beautifully, and the aroma of the gourmet food neatly displayed was driving me to criminality. Although I knew the consequences of my actions, I deposited the whole turkey, followed by everything on the table, directly into the pillowcase. My friend and I ran as fast as we could from the scene of the crime. Finally, we took shelter in the shade of a large tree and devoured all we could like two wild animals. We then disposed of the evidence of the pillowcase still containing the leftovers.

By the time we returned, a group of priests had lined up all students. We were able to sneak in on time for a roll call that was followed by interrogation. This was it. A death sentence. I passed the test by acting calm, but unfortunately, when my little friend was approached, he wet his shorts. What a horrible moment. I knew then that I was in deep trouble. But secretly, I was so content that I had been able to eat a decent meal after many months of having to put up with boiled spinach, I barely had time to get myself ready for the punishment I was about to receive. My partner in crime implicated me and spilled the beans.

"Mettez vous a genoux!" Mon Père Zuick commanded. We were forced to get on our knees, kneeling on the hard concrete surface for hours. In addition, each of us received ten to fifteen lashes on the palm of our hands using thin green branches cut from the big tree. I paid a handsome price that day, but to this date, I do not regret the unthinkable invasion of the sacred space. I still remember the taste of the wonderful meal and the way we ate like hungry beasts.

I also received nurturing, even in this forbidding place with its grandfather clock. Mon Père Estepino motivated me. The heavyset Italian priest would tell me where I needed to improve—and the subjects where I excelled. He offered me books to read and helped me with mathematics, which was my weakest subject. He took an interest in me and taught me to believe in myself even more. He saw some spark in me—and he nurtured it the way a fertilizer does to plants.

When a man is sufficiently motivated, discipline will take care of itself.

—ALBERT EINSTEIN

Mon Père Marcel organized Easter egg hunts and read to us at lunch, since we were forbidden to speak. There were pockets of joy and fondness even in the barren world I found myself in.

Over the summer each year, I would return to Shiraz, feeling a bit like a stranger in the place of my birth. I was obtaining a world-class, rigorous education. I had been exposed to a different culture and a totally different environment. My friends were from across the globe, countries I'd barely heard of. It was difficult, then, to relate to the kids around me in Shiraz. I loved being surrounded by my family, and I took advantage of the hugs and affection of my mother, which I did miss, but I was an outsider in my own birthplace.

My boarding school had changed me forever. I got up at five o'clock in the morning—even though summer was a time to sleep in. I kept to myself at times. I was self-reliant in a way none of my friends were—a little man in a boy's gangly body. At the end of every summer, I was sent back to *L'étoile* du *Matin.* I always felt a pang as the plane took to the skies—each summer I had home cooking, my mother's fussing over me. But leaving no longer frightened me. I no longer dreaded it. I had, most importantly, faith in myself.

I assumed I would stay at my boarding school until I graduated. However, my wise grandfather saw that I was beginning to be uncomfortable in the jasmine-scented world of my Persian childhood. I was spending years away from Persian culture, from my family, and that beautiful place. He convinced my parents to bring me back to Shiraz to attend a private school for three to four years of high school. The idea was I would obtain my diploma and then leave again for a college in Europe. But this time, I would be old enough to carry some of my country and family's culture more deeply within me.

I can see now my Aga and father were trying to shape my experiences—some of which were harder than others. But at least for me, I choose to forget the bad and remember the lessons and love of those beautiful wonder years. Despite the sternness of some of my experiences and in a culture where my father and grandfather could not bring themselves to say the words "I love you," I knew they loved me. This knowing was deep and unshakable.

I prefer to remember the good—that positivity carries me through life. Today, I get up in the morning, and it doesn't matter whether it's raining or whether it's cold or it's hot. I rise and see a good morning, a morning of opportunity. I choose to seek joy.

So, following Aga's advice, I returned to Shiraz for the last three to four years of high school. And I had to start over, in a sense. I had to reconnect with old childhood friends—and because of my experiences, they seemed less mature and different from me. I had to make friends again. But while I was happy and content, and I was surrounded by the family I had missed very much while in the boarding school, I still knew I was not "home."

But still, I was curious, an observer of people. For example, my father was a high-ranking officer in the shah's army. Because of his connections, he interacted with the American army base in Shiraz, which had tens of thousands of soldiers. My family lived in a lovely home, but my father also had a second beautiful house with many rooms. He leased this house to an American general, and the U.S. Army made the house almost like an extension of the base, assigning the various rooms to different officers.

My father had introduced me to this American general, with a silver star and gold epaulets on his uniform. I was so impressed by his quiet strength that I would ride my bike and would go there every chance that I could get after five o'clock. I took any excuse to meet this general. He had a collection of pipes, and he would smoke his pipe, tamping down tobacco with a sandalwood and amber scent infused with vanilla. To this day, if I smell a certain pipe tobacco, it brings back that time. He really took a liking to me, and there I would practice my English.

After conversing with the general, I would ride my bike home before sunset. But as my third year at school in Shiraz drew to a close, I sensed I would be taking another journey—this one even farther from home. Despite Shiraz's beauty, its green valley, and mountains in the distance, I felt pulled into the world beyond.

Reflection Questions

1. What childhood lessons did you carry with you to adulthood?

2. What is "home" to you? Is it a place? A person? Something else?

3. Who were some of the people who taught you formative lessons you carried forward in your life?

4. Have you ever had to start over in a new place, new career, new job, new life? What did you learn about yourself when you did so?

5. If you could offer your younger self one piece of advice, what would it be?

CHAPTER TWO

The Empty Date

Not all who wander are lost.

—J. R. R. TOLKIEN

The time had come to say goodbye to my family again. I was headed to England in the swinging sixties. After the shelter of boarding school and my years with my family, I might as well have been going to Mars. In fact, Mars might have been less strange than the world of bell-bottoms, velvet shirts, and British rock and roll.

Unlike the little boy with sweets in his pockets when he left for boarding school, I was on my way to becoming a man. My father came to the airport with me, and he hugged me goodbye in his rather stiff, formal way. Then he handed me a hardcover book in which he had written the date of my departure and a note of good luck—but also a space where my return date would be written one day. Yet, standing in the airport, people lugging suitcases, porters calling out, little children straggling behind parents and grandparents, I tuned it all out—and discerned that I was not coming back to Iran.

The date of return would be blank forever.

And deep down I knew that. However, I cannot tell you why or how. My father still envisioned a certain future for me. My father wanted me to be educated in England and then go to the United States to ultimately obtain my doctorate before utilizing all my cultural exposures and language skills—and one day return to Iran as a high-ranking diplomat. That was *his* dream for me. But all along, Iran, to me, was the place of my birth but not my destiny.

Sometimes, that kind of insight is painful. Perhaps we are not ready to face something. I have always faced obstacles head-on, however, and England was going to present me with new challenges.

Once at Brestford College, living and schooling in Margate near Canterbury in the province of Kent, and London, I was again around students from all over the globe. My main goal there was to advance my "English"—and I use those quotes there as my English was OK, but now I would become fluent. I would also learn a great deal about life itself.

I was around some very wealthy students, and I had friends whose parents sent them generous allowances. But I was beginning to understand that my upbringing from the boarding school meant I insisted on standing on my own two feet. I was loathe to accept help from my parents.

In return for becoming a man and learning to live on my own, I was rewarded.

With freedom.

I had been raised in a very rigid, strict, disciplined, and ascetic environment. This set me apart from others—so it was a blessing but at the same time isolating. Once I was in England, it was the first time that I could make decisions completely on my own. Did I want to go out and drink—party all the time? Did I want to study? Did I want to learn?

In England, for the first time, my life was not dictated by the rising of the sun and the morning Mass or by my parents. My life was my own. If I wanted to go out and indulge, I could. If I wanted to spend time with girls, no one was there to tell me to study instead. I pushed my boundaries—and yet, the discipline I had already learned, the pride I had in earning my own money, meant despite London's swinging sixties, and a world that was rapidly evolving, I still carried the values ingrained in me.

My family in Iran was comfortable, but many of my peers were extremely wealthy. By contrast, I did not arrive in England by private jet. I wasn't zipping around London on the weekends in an Aston Martin. My background gave me a true appreciation for the gift of education my family made possible for me, as well as the small allowance I was given. I basically tried very, very hard in that duration of time to learn as much as I could about the culture of others. I worked to speak the English language as beautifully as I could. But bear in mind, I grew up with a native tongue of Farsi and then speaking French, taught by Swiss, Armenian, Italian, and French priests. My accent is consequently unique.

Another gift I have carried with me through my whole life from these journeys far from home is the ability to be surrounded by a group of people from all over the world and to treat everyone with acceptance and equality, as well as to respect other cultures. That ability—to be comfortable in my own self while simultaneously being comfortable around others—has been another key to my success and also my happiness.

Because one believes in oneself, one doesn't try to convince others. Because one is content with oneself, one doesn't need others' approval. Because one accepts oneself, the whole world accepts him or her.

—LAO TZU

I also spent quite a bit of time observing others—I became a man at an early age through being sent far from home as just a small child. Along the way, I learned maturity is not an automatic result of age (I know plenty of adults who still have tantrums like children—and I am sure you do too). It was a blessing for me to accelerate the maturation process and to understand what life was all about. I knew already how to stand on my own two feet. Seeing some of the wealthy students around me, I knew I was not going to rely on the checks that I received from my parents. My classmates relied on monthly stipends that afforded them fine meals, fancy cars, and, later, elegant flats. For me, to expect my parents to do that somehow would be a sign of weakness.

My friend Hassan, whom we called Monty, and I boarded with a family near our college. Freedom may have been what I found in England, but in this case, we had a strict woman who took in boarders from the school and restricted just how much we, as growing young men, could eat. Our meals were rather meager and plain. In addition, her son was what I can only refer to as a pest.

Calling to mind my thievery of the priests' prized meal, Monty and I, stomachs growling, would raid the refrigerator late at night. While we tried to make what we took inconspicuous, our landlady always knew—and made sure we were aware of just how angry she was. But a hungry stomach trumps fear.

I certainly was not without youthful misadventures with my first taste of freedom. I bought myself a Morris Mini Minor in London for about £45. The car was what I think of as a very British green—mixed with rust. And it was completely unreliable—in fact, barely operational.

Now, for me, at that time, £45 would virtually tap me out. I realized if I spent all that money, I would not have enough for gas or repairs. So, I convinced a classmate to share the cost with me to be able to get this car. Each of us drove it. I think if we had tried to polish out the rust, the car would have simply disintegrated. The driver's seat had a most uncomfortable spring that inflicted pain every time we drove over a bump. To protect our poor bottoms, we took a throw pillow and placed it on the driver's seat. Ingenuity trumps discomfort. Problem solved.

While I recall that car fondly, more than once we were left stranded by the roadside when our Green Machine broke down. True story: Later, when I eventually left England for New York, I parked the car in the street with the keys in it and walked away. I'd love to know what its next adventure was! I hope whoever took it had a throw pillow.

Another scrape I got into in England was when a good friend of mine, Freddy, started dancing with this gorgeous young blond woman. After years of confining rules in boarding school, I was reveling in small freedoms as well as big. I was perfectly content sitting there drinking beer underage; for me, that was enough excitement. Then the energy of the nightclub changed as skinheads tromped in as if they owned the place, leather, piercings, bald heads, tattoos, and sneers. This was closing in on the seventies when London was exploding with rock music, outrageous fashions (a *lot* of ugly plaid), and young people full of expression against the old guard. From Pink

Floyd to David Bowie, from rising feminism to national strikes and new political parties, London was changing—and so was the world.

The skinheads immediately looked for trouble, and unfortunately, my friend Freddy found it. Apparently, the beautiful girl he had been so instantly enamored of was dating one of the skinheads. Chaos erupted. It was horrible. They broke my friend's nose—and meanwhile, I had dived under the table. This was certainly different from life with Mon Père Zuick. I wondered what the reserved and self-contained priest would have thought of my adventures in England.

And though I had freedom, it was still my nature to do everything on my own. Accepting help was a foreign concept to me—like showing up to the priest with a bloody nose and him asking me what could be done. The message was, solve it yourself. This remains true to this day because though you can ask for wise advice and counsel from friends and colleagues, in the end, you must determine where your path, where the solution, lies.

Because I began to really understand this principle of self-reliance, I remember a particular, very cold winter. I was renting a flat with friends. Back then (and still in some places), English heat was controlled through a small box in your flat. If you put coins in, the electric heat turned on. Heat is a necessary comfort in the often-damp English winters that chill you deep in your bones.

One very, very cold spell, I can remember going through couch cushions, every pocket I had—every pocket my roommates had. But the fact was, we were out of money. Outside, it was snowing like mad, and the chill permeated the damp house. I will confess—I broke the box on the wall. I took the money out of there. And I kept repeating the same shilling, over and over to stay warm. And then at the end of the month, I confessed my theft to the landlord.

"I want to be honest with you. I did it because of desperation." I confided in him, quite embarrassed. We had, between the roommates, pulled together some money by then, and I told him we were sorry and would pay for the cost of fixing the lock. However, the man appreciated my honesty and told me it was all right.

Another lesson learned: Honesty truly is the best policy.

One concept I have absorbed over and over throughout my life is that there is a man in the mirror. I've worked with countless people, met many countless more, but there is one person I am ultimately accountable to. Myself. The man in the glass. Knowing that, I can truthfully say that I have moved through my life always striving to stay faithful to that person.

At the conclusion of my prep-school education in England, though, it was time for another journey. It seemed each journey I made, each path, took me further from the place of my birth. This time, I was off to cross the Atlantic Ocean. I was headed to a country I pictured as one where you could make your own fortune, master of your own destiny—I was next being sent to America to continue my education.

Unfortunately, I thought I was quite clever, and I decided to do some gambling. I planned to take my modest savings and multiply it at one of the many slot machines displayed at every bowling alley and bar in Margate. Also, unfortunately, I was naïve to the fact that the house always wins. The odds are very much stacked in their favor—no matter how clever I might have thought I was with cards or the "luck" (or lack thereof) of the roulette wheel.

Thus, my little nest egg withered away at the casino—and I was off to New York City with a mere $450 in my pocket—and the name and address of a distant cousin.

Now, Persian culture is unique in how it views family, as well as its desire for impeccable manners. First, it is considered a "blessing" for your family and friends to show up unannounced. You will see more than once in this book that this is not *always* such a wonderful thing. While family is a blessing, knowing they are coming is kind of essential, especially in busy modern life. In addition, as in many cultures, the definition of "family" can include fourth cousins twice removed or other very distant kin.

At this time, however, I was not aware of this colossally inconvenient thing my parents had done by sending me to this man. Meanwhile, a friend from school in London and I agreed to fly to New York together to help each other out. Sherry, journeying from Europe to America, alone as a single woman, thought traveling with me would be safer. We were friends, not romantic partners, but I was happy to look out for her.

She and I arrived at John F. Kennedy Airport late at night, in bitter weather, landing to the sight of piles of dirty snow from snowplows pushing the wet stuff off the tarmac and parking lots. This was in a different era of airline travel when you could meet your incoming party at their gate. We walked up the carpeted jetway, and I assumed my cousin would be waiting there for us. Instead, we entered the airport, which was deserted, gates drawn down on shops. So, we trudged to the baggage claim area for international flights. Again, I expected my distant cousin to be waiting for us—almost like a limo driver waiting with their name signs at the gates of an airline.

I also did not actually know what my cousin looked like. I assumed he would look vaguely like me, like a fellow Persian. I stood and scanned the small gathering of people waiting for passengers as I descended the escalator. But no sight of a cousin who resembled me.

Back then, pre-cell phones, you could page people in airports, so I went to the courtesy phone and requested that. His name was bleated out over the speakers. No sign of my cousin.

Sherry and I looked around. We got our bags. We waited until the baggage claim area was completely desolate with only a night janitor for company. With a sinking feeling, I realized my cousin was not coming. Ever the optimist, I knew he was a doctor, so I thought, *Perhaps he has had a medical emergency he must attend to.*

I had his address in my pocket, and though it was late and I had no idea where we were going, we hailed a yellow cab to take us to New York City and the street number scribbled in the letter my mother had sent me. I made every effort to appear as if I knew all about New York—as I had heard stories of out-of-towners being taken circuitous routes and charged triple for cab rides. I also felt I needed to be the "man"—after all, I was supposed to be protecting my friend, Sherry. Meanwhile, according to the manners of the day, I would not let her pay for half the cab—or anything. So, my money was dwindling before I even got to my cousin's.

Off we went into the night. I gave the cabbie the address. My friend leaned her head against the back seat and dozed, while I took in my new city and country. I had, of course, come from London, but New York has its own unique energy, and the skyscrapers are impressive. It also never sleeps—the cliché is true.

Meanwhile, I should add for detail that my parents had given me a single winter jacket made out of sheepskin and leather. I had it turned sheepskin out (for what did I know of fashion). So, I had arrived in New York City dressed as a sheep. I am quite certain the cabbie was wise to the fact that I was from abroad and not a street-savvy New Yorker or city person at all. Nonetheless, he took us straight to my cousin's address.

The cabbie pulled up in front of Mount Sinai—a prominent New York hospital. I stared outside at the entrance to the building. "Sir, you're wrong. This cannot be the address. I'm going to my cousin's apartment."

This New York cabbie did not care about my dilemma. In fact, he turned around with a murderous stare and said, "I don't really give a *&#@ about your cousin. Get out of my damn cab now!"

This was my welcome to New York City and to the United States. This was so different from the environments I had been in. But I am nothing if not adaptable!

Sherry and I retrieved our bags from the trunk of the cab, climbed over the slush and blowing newspaper pages and trash in the gutter, and stood on the sidewalk of the hospital. There was only one thing to do. Track down my cousin, who I'd been told was a famous doctor.

We entered the hospital, thankful to get out of the bitter night air. I walked over to the information desk and asked the woman if she could point me to my cousin, giving her his name.

She looked at me as if I had just arrived from a turnip farm and said, "I have no idea who Dr. So-and-so is."

I informed her he was famous. Surely she knew him.

She gave me an imperious look over the glasses on the bridge of her nose. "They're all famous."

I pleaded my case. I nodded toward my tired friend, Sherry, and explained we had just landed from England and that there was a mix-up. "I need to find my cousin, and my parents have accidentally given me his work address."

She pointed to some hard plastic seats under flickering fluorescent lights. "If I were you, I would go over there to the waiting area and just sit there and watch until you recognize him."

This was not the advice I was hoping for.

She added, "If you don't recognize him, I'm sorry … I can't help you."

Well, at least she hadn't cursed me out like the cabbie. Perhaps our luck was changing.

Sherry had by now staked out two side-by-side chairs and had curled up, sound asleep. I sat there and stayed awake, scanning every person who came that potentially resembled a Persian in a doctor coat. Finally, at around eight in the morning or eight-fifteen, I spotted a man heading toward the elevators, and his profile somehow gave me the impression that this was the man. I called out his name—and sure enough, he turned around.

I explained that his mother had talked to mine, and I was given his name and address for a place to stay when I arrived in New York. I could tell, as the color in his face drained, that no one had informed him.

"I never got such a message. And now, I am afraid, I have surgery."

He was stone-faced, but he had a suggestion. "This is the best I can do right now. I am going to give you the keys to my car. It is in the parking lot on the sixth floor, and it's a green car. I'm parked about three spots from the end." He described the make and model to me. "You can go and sleep in the car until my shift is over around five-thirty."

If my parents only knew how badly this had turned out. With little choice, I accepted the keys and informed Sherry. We trudged out to the parking deck in the absolute freezing cold, with periodic icy rain. We located the car. Then we went and found a pizza-by-the-slice spot as we were ravenously hungry. Pizza by the slice was not a thing in England, and I have never been more appreciative of a slice of pizza in my life. We headed back to the green car, trudging through the bad weather, both exhausted. I was too embarrassed to run the engine, so we shivered and ached and waited for my cousin.

He showed up in the darkness of the early-sunset winter and was clearly less than pleased. He informed me that his apartment was undergoing construction because of a leak and it was out of the question to host us. I thought this was about as real an excuse as saying Santa Claus was already sleeping on the couch. Then he offered to take us to his brother—a college student. Perhaps *this* cousin could put us up.

We drove for forty-five minutes and arrived at a not-very-nice apartment shared by four college students. The doctor informed his brother we were distant cousins and to take care of us, and then left without so much as a goodbye. We ended up spending the night sleeping on a very dirty carpet. So much for protecting my friend, Sherry, from the indignities of New York City.

That was my welcome to the United States of America! But my journey was really just starting.

Reflection Questions

1. When did you first experience freedom to make your own decisions?

2. What do our youthful mistakes and misadventures teach us? What lessons have you learned from your own first steps into adulthood?

3. Whether in business or personal life, honesty is usually the best policy. Can you think of a professional situation in which things went awry, but being truthful about it meant you ultimately prevailed?

4. How comfortable are you with the person in the mirror?

5. Have you ever felt your destiny was different from the path you were on?

CHAPTER THREE

Education—in the School of Life

Formal education will make you a living;
self-education will make you a fortune.
—JIM ROHN

New York had not rolled out its red carpet for me. Or perhaps it did, and that was just a New York City–style carpet. Since I, of course, was not going to call home to Iran and tell my parents my misfortunes (or ask for money), I knew I needed to quickly figure out what I was going to do.

After three nights on the very smelly carpet of a frat-boy apartment, I told Sherry, "Look, why don't we just go ahead and rent an apartment? We can basically get on with our lives and not have to rely or depend on anybody."

Self-reliance was now so ingrained in me that I would never have pictured doing otherwise.

Meanwhile, off I went to register at Queensborough College. Standing in line at the registrar's office, I was making conversation with the person next to me, explaining how I had just come from

England and my misfortunes since arrival. The guy I was talking to started chuckling while also assuring me he felt badly for my situation. All of a sudden, this other guy taps my shoulder and says, "I understand that you are without housing. Let me tell you, I've been here for many years, and I live with my girlfriend, and we are moving to a much bigger house. We are giving up our apartment, which if you like, you can take over the rent. I'll show it to you after you finish registering if you want."

I thought this was a godsend. After I registered, we took two buses to this apartment. On the way there, he explained it would cost $280 to collect up front, and then Sherry and I would pay the rent from that point on directly to the landlord.

The place was perfect for what we needed. We agreed to the deal, and then I went to find Sherry, and each of us took our stuff and headed to the apartment. We were so thrilled that, along the way, we stopped at a W. T. Grant's department store to buy pillows and some blankets—no more itchy, ugly carpet-bed.

Still exhausted from all we had been through since landing in New York, we fell asleep—her in the bedroom and me in the living room. But then at six-thirty the next morning, someone was trying to break in the front door. This was like I had been warned about New York! I bolted upright but realized it wasn't a break-in. The person had a key—and in walked a very large man with a sizable belly and a woolen cap on his head. He barked, "What the hell is going on here?!"

I bolted to my feet. "Sir, we've rented this place. It's our apartment." By this time, Sherry stood sleepily in the doorway to the bedroom, her face slowly registering alarm. I said to the intruder, "What are *you* doing here?"

"I own this place!"

"Own it? What do you mean you own this place?" I explained my story from the beginning—from landing in JFK to the smelly frat-house apartment to my good fortune in finding the man to rent this apartment from.

"I evicted that son of a bitch a month ago for not paying his rent!"

I felt queasy. I was not yet even twenty years old—still a teenager, now completely broke, an ocean and thousands of miles from Iran, with no one to turn to, in the midst of lousy weather and no obvious solution. In short, I was devastated.

The landlord growled, "You've got fifteen minutes to pack up and get out of here." He glanced at his watch. "Clock's ticking."

Sherry just crumbled. She sank into the ground and cried.

I said to the man, "You know what, I don't know you from Adam, but you look like a nice man." (This was a white lie, I admit!) "Could you help me because I have nowhere to go?"

He looked at me, and he saw that I was real—that I meant it. I now know to be successful, and you too must recognize honesty and realness when it's looking you in the face. This man knew I had been had in a big way. He said, "Look, I can do something for you. Do you have $180?"

I was burning through most of my own money. I conferred with Sherry. She put up some money (which I had been reluctant to do previously because of a sense of chivalry of the times). I put up some money. We handed it over to him, and I said an internal prayer that this guy was not also going to rip us off.

He counted it, nodded, and said, "Bring your luggage." He ended up connecting us with still another guy—a snowplow driver, no less, whose snowplow I followed, tromping along on old rock salt and slush. Sherry was in a long, black coat, and leather boots with high heels, so she sat on the bucket in front of the snowplow next to the luggage. I trudged behind, face blue, fingers frozen, with no idea where we were being led. However, this was a most unceremonious way to arrive.

After several hundred feet, we arrived at very large apartment complex, and we found out later that the large man who entered the apartment was not the owner—he was the super.

There was one little duplex on this property, set off a little. The plow driver, an assistant to the first guy, took us to a studio apartment directly above the boiler room. The floors were *hot.* The man said, "This is all I can give to you. But you can stay until you get yourself together and move to a new place."

The thing that always attracted me to New York was the sense of being in a place where a lot of people had a lot of stories not unlike mine.

—SALMAN RUSHDIE

In truth, looking around the shabby place that was all ours temporarily, I was grateful for this kindness. Sometimes angels don't arrive in halos but in greasy coveralls with a foul mouth.

However, I knew the first thing I needed to do was find a job—or I would end up in precisely the same place, about to be kicked out on the streets. I needed a job not just for my living expenses but also to ensure I could continue my education. I was in the United States on a student visa. If I was not in courses, I could be sent home. So, I needed to work both for my immigration status and for my own support. When I went to the campus later that afternoon, I searched until I found the guy who stole my money.

In fact, I found him—and then I surreptitiously followed him to his new place (where he was no doubt conning his next landlord).

I memorized the bus routes and then headed back to my very hot boiler-room apartment.

The next day, I retraced the route to the thief and arrived at his apartment. I rang the doorbell, already aware he would be on campus in classes. An attractive American girl answered. "What can I do for you, sir?"

With the slight glance afforded of the apartment through the semi-open door, I spotted a beautiful Persian carpet. I could tell it was the real deal and very valuable.

Thinking on my feet, I said, "Your boyfriend told me to come in and take up the Persian carpet because we need to have it cleaned." I knew enough about Persian carpets to toss out some phrases and then to say, "I am the only one at my company who knows how to clean this." She kindly agreed to let me, and I promptly rolled up the carpet and took it—on the bus no less. I sat in the back, carrying the carpet like a fat sausage, trying to ignore the stares of the other passengers.

I found the guy on campus yet again the next day. I walked directly up to him and said, "You bring my money back, and then you can have your carpet—and you're lucky that I did not call the police on you."

Fortunately, he was ultimately reasonable. He brought my money to me—which I desperately needed to keep going in this dog-eat-dog world of New York City. I gave him his carpet back. And I began to understand life on a different level. This was beyond learning freedom in England. This was *life* and how to survive.

Like a Horatio Alger story, I was (nearly) penniless, arriving to this great city with ambition, luck, and a healthy dose of stubbornness. It would take my wits to make it. But those same wits would help me through my whole life.

At college, I took as many classes as I could—just in case I ran out of money after a semester. I took the basics—English 101 and all those general courses. I was also introduced to philosophy. In fact, the first day that I took my philosophy class, the professor walked in and brought a chair to the front of the room. He set it down. Empty. He stood and leaned against the blackboard. I happened to be sitting up front because I wanted to be just like a sponge.

He gestured to the wooden chair and asked, "What do you see here?"

With all the arrogance a young man could muster, I said, "What? Are you kidding me? I'm looking at a chair."

He asked, "Are you sure?"

"Of course, I am sure. I can touch it. It's there. And it's a chair."

Then he started arguing that indeed, maybe that chair was next to him in the front of the room. But maybe the chair didn't exist.

In an instant, he opened an intellectual door that I had never, ever thought about. Is this an illusion? Are we all here? Do we exist? You know, the kinds of questions young people can mull over wine and conversation late into the night in dorm rooms and apartments the world over. From then until today, I have been fascinated with philosophy.

The unexamined life is not worth living.

—SOCRATES

I tried to look at my schedule and think, if I take night classes, I can work days. If I take day classes, I can work nights. Meanwhile, word had traveled on campus that another student tried to con me, and I had outsmarted him by taking his very expensive carpet. He was made fun of. But I also told my classmates the truth. My plea: "Listen,

I came from London with less than five hundred bucks. I almost lost most of it. I am living on top of a boiler room. I need a job or I can't stay—and I can't stay if I am not a student because of my visa. So, I need to both work *and* be a student."

Someone took pity on me. "If you want to work and you want to be absolutely guaranteed a job, this is the address you go to, and they will hire you. All you have to do is ask for George."

This sounded good, so I took two buses again. (I will say this for my experiences—I learned the bus lines!) I followed the directions to the address. It was a very industrial area of New York, reeking of motor oil and fumes, and with the building belching black smoke into the air.

I walked around to a door by the loading dock, and an absolutely huge guy with biceps the size of the circumference of my waist was standing on a concrete platform and staring at me. I informed him I was looking for George.

He started using profanity and then said, "You're looking at him. Now what do you want?"

I used the name of the person who had sent me there and said, "He told me that I can get a job with you."

George said, "OK, you're hired."

Now I was confused. He didn't even know my name. "I'm hired? What do I do?"

He never said to come in here and fill out an app. He never told me any of the stuff you normally associate with being hired. He asked me nothing. He intoned, "Follow me," and started inside.

I said, "Sir, my name is Paul."

He nodded. "From now on, you're George."

I said, "Yes, sir, no problem."

In fact, I think every single person who has lived any length of time in New York has a story like mine. New York is a place built for stories like this—full of cultures and characters. Either you become scrappy and make it or you head home with your proverbial tail between your legs. I was *not* going home.

He brought me into a factory that I promise the Occupational Safety and Health Administration (OSHA) had never been inside of. I trailed behind the man, who stopped in front of a massive, loud machine. "Hey, George," he said. "This is called a conveyor belt." And he's showing me a belt with pieces of equipment zooming down it. "You see this?"

"Yes, sir."

And he said, "You see those &#$@ing things right there?"

"Yes, sir," I replied and nodded sagely as if this was the most normal thing in the world.

"These transformers are on the conveyor belt, and the conveyor belt has a fast velocity, and these transformers travel very fast. Your job is to be at the end of the conveyor belt, and you have two options." (And by the way, I am leaving out the expletives in front of every other word out of his mouth.)

"Yes, sir," I again replied.

"Option one: you can let the transformer fall on your feet and break the heck out of your foot—and the transformer. You don't want that to happen, do you, George?"

"No, sir!"

"The second option that you have is to grab the transformer and put it in the box. That's all I want you to do."

I said, "Yes, sir, no problem." This sounded like an easy-enough job.

He took me to the conveyer belt where I would be working. And that conveyor belt was coming at me like the *I Love Lucy* episode where the chocolates are quickly coming down the factory line to Lucy and Ethel. Only in my case, these were no chocolates I could stuff in my mouth and under my hat but heavy transformers.

As they came at me, I grabbed them, put them in the box, grabbed them, put them in the box, grabbed them, put them in the box. At ten o'clock, a loud whistle blew over all of the factory for the short break, and all the workers stopped. Everyone stepped outside for a smoke—even if they weren't smokers. The factory workers puffed away, a cloud of smoke above them all. I quietly walked to the front entrance, took a bus, and never went back. And I never collected a paycheck, which meant that I *still* needed to find a job.

I answered an ad for a place on Jamaica Avenue underneath the elevated trains. I sure hoped it wasn't another factory, but it turned out to be a furniture store. The manager there asked me, "Do you wanna work, kid?"

At this point, I had visions of having to go home to Iran—something I deep down refused to entertain. I said, "Yes, sir."

Realizing this was a furniture store, I added, "I'm a good salesman." (Of course, I had never sold anything in my life!)

He looked at me. "I don't want you to sell furniture. I have another job for you."

It turned out that there was a large parking lot across the street, which he owned in addition to the furniture store. He offered me a flat rate—I can't recall how much, but even if it was $40 a day, that felt like a veritable fortune to me. The building across the street attached to the parking lot was the welfare office. My job was to collect the money for parking for the people using the lot as they visited the welfare department and then to mend, take care of, and look after the parking lot in whatever way was necessary.

This was the quintessential hardened New Yorker. He warned me, "I'm gonna go and count every car every day. And you give me the money for that number of cars. If they don't give you the money for any reason, if you are stupid and don't collect money from someone, it's not my problem. You need to come up with the shortfall."

This guy sounded like a strict boss. But this was better than grabbing transformers for George. So, I agreed on the spot and felt rich as a king that night, knowing I had money coming in. For three months, I ran the business and had it operating efficiently. I made sure the parking lot was clean, no trash blowing around. I was respectful to every person who parked their car. I was taking multiple classes, and so, for me, this job allowed me to work around my schedule.

By the third month, as a man of business (because I was learning at each step of the way), I observed some of the other businesses around us, including a car wash. At the time, "Simonizing"—a form of detailing cars that was popular in the 1970s—was a buzzword. I realized that I could polish cars in the time that people were inside the government building. With my manners, I would politely ask, "Madam, sir, would you like your car Simonized?" (This, despite my not being 100 percent sure what Simonizing actually entailed.)

So, I would collect the money for the parking lot, just as my boss expected. I never shorted him so much as a dollar (even after he started to trust me and didn't check so carefully). Then I would charge ten bucks or more to "Simonize," take the car to the car wash, pay ninety-nine cents for a wash, dry it extra shiny, and return it to the car owners.

Eventually, my little side hustle expanded so well that I went back and recruited six college students, including my two best friends,

Freddy and Monty. I put them on my "payroll" at two bucks or three bucks an hour, whatever it was I was paying them. These employees of mine were responsible for taking the car to the carwash and then drying and rubbing it with a chamois afterward. Now, imagine, I had no insurance or anything. Nonetheless, my business boomed. My employees—most of them friends and acquaintances—all got tips when they returned the cars to their owners. We were all making more money than we had in our lives.

Within six months' time, my life was changing. I moved to an apartment with Freddy, Monty, Sherry, and Abraham. The latter was a rather eccentric fellow—who didn't always pay the bills (our electricity got shut off more than once!). In fact, Abraham was the cause of yet another misadventure in New York. I was dating a fellow student named Karen who was taking classes to become a writer. All I wanted was a little alone time with her—despite living with roommates. So, I did what any college kid would do—I bribed them.

I paid off each of my roommates to leave me alone for the night, and I had candles ready and opened a bottle of wine. I went to my room to change, and when I came back, my roommate Abe was sitting there on the couch. Now, there is no polite way to say this: Abe was pretty disgusting. He was an engineering major, a true genius but without any sense of personal hygiene.

How bad was he? He'd wear his socks so many days in a row, they would be stiff like a pair of boots. Abe was not part of my evening plans. He was sitting there watching television, and I reminded him, "You were supposed to be gone. We had a deal."

He was Turkish, and his communication skills in English were not yet fluent. But he did know some words, including, "It will cost you money." So, I gave him $20 to leave. And twenty bucks was plenty of money from me back then. Then he complained that he had nowhere to go because he did not have a car. Reluctantly, I loaned him the keys to my car.

At last, my stinky roommate was gone, and Karen and I were sitting there, talking over wine, jazz playing in the background. It was wonderful just to be with her, most especially without a bunch of roommates hanging about. All of a sudden, the house phone rang, and it was the police department. They informed me my car had been impounded.

"Impounded?"

"Yes, sir, and the guy who was driving it claims that you lent the car to him. And his name is Abraham."

"What the heck did he do? What do you mean impounded? What does that mean?"

What it meant, of course, is that I had to rush there—and it was going to cost me money—money that I did not have. Not only that, the officer informed me that if I didn't get there soon, the car would be impounded until the next day—and it would cost me even more money.

Our date ruined, Karen drove me to the police station. We had to post some money to get Abraham out and then more money for the car. Karen loaned me the cash—which embarrassed me to no end.

And what had Abraham done? He had taken my $20 and gone to a dive bar to drink. He bought a round for an attractive woman sitting next to him, which impressed her. They started chatting and hit it off. He invited her to go for a ride—in my car, of course. As they were driving, he said, "This is a lot of fun. Would you like to go out with me tomorrow?"

She smiled and patted his thigh. "Sure, but it will cost you a hundred bucks."

Abraham, of course, now realized she was a call girl. He had not planned on this, and so he rapidly pulled over to let her out with a "no, thank you."

As luck would have it—or lack of luck, as it was—as he was letting her out on the sidewalk, a cop car pulled up at the back of him. They picked her up for soliciting; he was driving without a license—and I was too broke to get my car out of impound without Karen's help.

I made up my mind then and there that I would never have anyone loan me money ever again. I wanted to stand on my own two feet—as I had been, not letting my parents and family in Iran know all of the adventures and misadventures, hardships, setbacks, and good fortunes that I had been experiencing in America.

I found the whole thing very embarrassing. Karen and I laughed, but it was sad at the same time. Of course, I paid her back and took care of my obligations, but when you are poor, sometimes you end up doing things that really you may not want to do or you may never choose. These lessons stuck with me—and have also given me compassion toward others who are struggling.

Struggling or not, though, to me, to all of us, the apartment was a huge step up—no more stinky carpet (stinky roommate, yes; stinky rug, no), no more boiler-room heat.

Meanwhile, I was about to expand my entrepreneurship. Each week, this heavyset fellow parked his Cadillac, and he would have my so-called company wash his car. He was an employee in the welfare department.

One day, he said, "Paul, I am thinking of selling my car."

I inquired as to the price. I think it was about $2,500. I calculated how much money I could scrape together—and there was no way I would be able to buy it. But I did my best sales pitch. "Listen, I'm a student. I don't have any money. You know what I do for a living—and I do take extra good care of your car every week."

He was very nice, and he sold the car to me much cheaper than he wanted to sell to anybody else. Soon, I was the proud owner of a burgundy two-door Cadillac with a blacktop. I no longer had to take buses and subways to get to my job. When I took possession, I told my employees, "A very important man owns this Cadillac. I want you to clean it and detail it—miss nothing!"

And so they did, and when they saw *I* was the man who owned the car, they knew I'd pulled a prank on them. I am still friends with Monty—and he *still* does not let me forget that I made him detail my car.

As a young entrepreneur (which is what I was, even if my businesses were those of a young man hustling to find his fortune), I began to realize that I needed to expand and that I needed to go way beyond what I was doing. My nature was to always be on a quest for the next success—and that has also helped me. I think of the next challenge and the next. Whether it is running a side hustle car cleaning business or running projects with hundreds of millions of dollars.

The owner of the furniture store was also an observant gentleman. He came to me and said, "I can see you are very intelligent. I want you to come and work in the furniture store." That was what I had wanted to do in the first place. New York winters were, as I already knew, rather bitter, and being inside would be far more pleasant than running the car park. Ever the entrepreneur, I passed along running my "business" to my friend (who is now a multimillionaire in Newport Beach, showing, I think, the seeds of success are in some of us from early on). Meanwhile, I now took a cut of operations.

I was working, obviously, in the furniture store right across the street. I had a business mindset—I hadn't built up that business to watch it fall apart. During lulls in the day, I would walk across the street and check out operations, making sure they were doing a good job and taking care of the customer base I had built up (because if you don't have exceptional customer relations, you have nothing). I began to understand what it means to expand businesses. I started to understand diversification—I now had income coming from more than one source.

My employees were thrilled with their jobs. I treated them fairly and tried to train them to give a solid customer experience to maximize their tips. However, I also noticed that none of the employees who worked with me had the same sort of entrepreneurial drive. I was figuring out what set me apart from my peers.

Meanwhile, my boss at the furniture store put my new job to me in this way: "Paul, I'm not going to pay you a base wage. I am going to put you on a commission. If you succeed, you will make more money than you have ever made. If you don't, you will be broke. It's sink or swim."

By now, from hustling for car washes, I was an exceptional salesman. I was assigned to sell mattresses. Now, I will say that *furniture* (sofas and living room sets) was his biggest sales department. I was starting out in the unexciting bed department. I didn't just sell mattresses though—I sold experiences. If someone came in to purchase a bed, I would ask them to take their shoes off.

"Lie down here, on this mattress. Close your eyes. Picture yourself lying in this bed after a very long day at your job. Imagine how well you will sleep."

In essence, I told them a bedtime story. I began to sell more beds and more mattresses than this owner had ever sold in his life. He offered credit for people who did not have enough to purchase their furniture outright. He was making money. I was making money. I was an entrepreneur on the side, and I was on my way. But I still had new ambitions. Another friend of mine (the benefits of networking!) said, "Paul, on weekends, I'm working at this place called the White Horse. If you have experience as a waiter, you could make a lot of money."

I had faith in my ability to learn anything quickly and to adapt. Thus, I told a white lie. I said, "Sir, in England, I worked as a waiter. One of the best." Actually, it was not a white lie—it was an actual lie. Of course, this was before the day of email and internet and any way to check such a claim. However, he didn't even need to do that. He knew that I was full of it.

"Do you know how to serve seafood?"

"Of course!"

Meanwhile, I knew nothing about seafood—Iran is a central desert plateau.

My night was a bit of a disaster. Lobster was being served. In came a man straight out of central casting—corpulent and mumble-mouthed. He ordered lobster—and requested a "BBBmbib."

Or something like that.

I asked him to repeat himself, and he muttered again, "BEEEbmbmb."

In fact, this man, one of the White Horse's top customers, was growing more and more irate when I was not showing up at the table with his requested item.

Eventually, frantic, I raced into the kitchen and hoped the chef would take pity on me. "He wants a bbbbmb! What does he want?"

I am lucky the chef did not take a meat cleaver to me. It turned out, of course, that the poor customer wanted a LOBSTER BIB! But as I had clearly lied about my experience in a seafood restaurant, that was both my first and last night on the job. I was so embarrassed I did not even return for my one night's paycheck.

But this disastrous night did not deter me. By the time, I was in my second year of college, I had taken all my basic classes, and in my mind, it was time to get more serious about my fortunes. In Queens, New York, there was a place called Terrace on the Park. It was a large T-shaped structure that had originally been built as a heliport for the 1964 World's Fair. It now was a fancy wedding and catering venue. They probably held twenty or thirty weddings each month. More in June.

I worked Friday and Saturday nights and took Sundays to study—I was still on that student visa.

Soon, I was making so much money and putting savings aside. It would be hard to spend it because it seemed all I did was study and work.

Queens, and New York in general, is such a mix of cultures and traditions. To me, this was like winning the lottery! And my hourly wage was before tips. Because of my excellent manners, formed in a strict environment, with "yes, ma'am" and "yes, sir," my tips were always above all others.

At the Terrace, the Italian weddings were the absolute best. Such happiness (who doesn't love a wedding). Excellent tips. (Happy people tip much better than unhappy people!) I tried to get myself booked for the Italian weddings. And then the managers saw in me a desire to succeed, a way of dealing with the customers and ensuring each wedding was as perfect as we could make it. So, rather quickly, they made me a captain.

Now I was in charge of the waiters and the bartenders. I used the same thinking, work ethic, and the like as I used at the car wash. Be exceptional—give the very best service possible.

As the captain, the weddings I worked always got the highest tip amount. We did a tip share. At the end of the night, we distributed our wealth—and soon I was the captain everyone wanted to work under. I worked at the Terrace on the Park, perched high above Flushing Meadow Park with a view of the skyline of Manhattan for almost a year and a half.

However, in my improbable journey, fate was about to intervene again.

I still had my Cadillac. And now I had money saved up. Monty convinced me that the next step in my education was far from New York. At that moment in time, I was a young man—and he asked, "What are you most interested in?"

My answer was *girls.*

And where could two young guys find girls? My friend told me: Florida. We made plans to transfer to Marymount College in Florida (now called Lynn University in Boca Raton). Warm weather? Beaches? Bikinis? What more could I want? I had my Cadillac, and so, of course, we were going to drive this car straight down I-95 until we reached our destination.

We stopped to refuel at some point on the way. As we stood next to the gas pump, in pulled a Porsche 914. If you are unfamiliar with cars, this was a Porsche made from 1969 to 1976 in conjunction with Volkswagen. A little rag-tipped sportster. *Very* small. And, in this case, very *orange*.

It must have been about three o'clock in the morning, and the very large gentleman driving the tiny car lumbered out, filled his tank, and then bought a pack of cigarettes at the convenience store attached to the station. My friend, Monty, who was traveling with me in his own convertible Mustang, was in the restroom, and the man from the Porsche said, "Hey, buddy, I love your car."

Now, because of the films we occasionally got to see in boarding school—and my own interests—I *loved* fast cars. I replied, "Wow, I love your car."

"Well, I wish I hadn't bought this." (Now, at the time I was less than 150 pounds, and this man was much larger, and I could see his point. This tiny orange car's driver's seat could barely accommodate him.)

"I wish I could have bought myself a Cadillac like yours."

Always quick on my feet, I proposed a deal, "I'll tell you what … I would love a car like yours, even though this Cadillac drives like a dream. I love sports cars. How about I give you my pink slip [title] and you give me yours. You are happy. I am happy. We each go on our merry way."

He looked at me and asked, "Are you serious?"

"I am," I said resolutely.

His car, by the way, was brand new—maybe three weeks old.

And in the middle of the night, we did it. We agreed to swap the pink slips. The next day, we met up to properly make the exchange with the DMV. I took the little Porsche that I loved. And he took my Cadillac. I was now driving in a tiny orange—but awesome—car to the next phase of my adventures.

However, I think some of my more unbelievable instances of luck or fate were really born by never being held back by doubts and always being open to the universe. I never step anywhere in fear. I step forward in faith that it will all work out.

So many people who saw the movie *Good Will Hunting* recall a scene when the janitor character played by Matt Damon solves an "impossible" equation on a blackboard. Not all people know that this is at least somewhat based on George Dantzig.[1] He was a mathematician who showed up late to class one day.

On the board were a couple of problems—one of which was considered impossible to solve: an unsolvable equation, more mythical to most mathematicians than practical. George Dantzig, however, mistook it for homework.

And he solved it.

He solved an equation that had stumped the geniuses of mankind before him. Later, Dantzig conceded that had he known it was "unsolvable" instead of a homework assignment, he would have given up. The lesson, of course, is that sometimes our *mind* cages us. We think things can't be done. So, we don't.

My experiences through my whole life, and especially once I arrived in America, were that nothing was impossible. I was open to all experiences, to all the world had to offer me. I was not confined by self-doubt or by expectations.

And, in Florida, my life was going to change in significant ways. But meanwhile? I had a fast little Porsche to take me there.

---

1 Matt Davis, "Remembering George Dantzig: The real Will Hunting," March 29, 2019, accessed July 1, 2022, https://bigthink.com/high-culture/george-dantzig-real-will-hunting/#:~:text=How%20the%20story%20of%20a,protagonist%20of%20Good%20Will%20Hunting.&text=One%20of%20the%20iconic%20scenes,he%20works%20as%20a%20janitor.

Reflection Questions

1. Attention to customers and good service to them can be traced from mowing lawns to delivering newspapers to running multiple companies. What can you say about your commitment to unparalleled customer experiences?

2. Chance encounters have changed my life. How have they changed yours? How have you taken advantage of fate?

3. I sold the customers of the furniture shop an "experience." How can connecting with clients on a deeper level enhance your sales?

4. What do you think are the traits of an entrepreneur?

5. I thought outside the box when assigned to manage a parking lot. Outside-the-box thinking isn't confined to the upper echelons of the C-suite. It is a mindset. What is a time that you thought outside the box?

CHAPTER FOUR

Written in the Stars

Important encounters are planned by the souls long before the bodies see each other.

—PAULO COELHO

I wish I could say it was the love of learning that (at first) brought me to the sunny shores of Florida.

But I was young. And so, if I am truthful, it was girls.

I could have stayed in the Northeast to pursue my degree. Or head to the College of Boca Raton, which ended up accredited as part of the University of Delaware. Like any young person, not yet twenty, I chose to head south down I-95 in my new-to-me Porsche to the land of sunshine, bikinis, sandy beaches, blue skies, and nightlife—it is easy to see why Florida won.

I studied but did not fully apply myself. I needed to keep a course load for my visa, but I was an interested if indifferent student. I could skate along and pass without being too challenged. I am not sure that any calling was yet emerging.

One day a professor of mine asked me to come and meet with him. He took me to the professors' dining room and invited me to order whatever I wanted. I got a burger—as a "hungry" college kid, I remember being excited by the prospect.

Then he turned to me, very seriously, and asked, "Why are you here?"

I had food in my mouth and gestured that I could not speak until I finished my bite.

He looked satisfied, as if he had just proved a point. "You must have been raised in a proper way because a lot of people would just speak with their mouth full."

I told him about my unique experiences, how rigid the Catholic boarding school was, and how young I had been when I was sent there.

He peered at me across the table. "If you are so disciplined, why are you not studying hard? You're intelligent; you have ambition. And you are chasing girls more than you study."

I had an "aha" moment. I suppose some of us, in late adolescence or our early twenties, are more "in the moment"; we work and play in our own little bubble. I had never considered what this professor said before.

I told him how grateful I was that he brought it to my attention. And I meant it. If someone tells you something about yourself that is truth, don't avoid it. Face it.

"Paul, I want you to study hard. And I want you to go places in life because I know you will succeed. And when you do, send me a postcard."

I shook his hand and appreciated his advice—and that he saw something in me. Self-belief and the belief of others can propel someone forward. I know many people would dismiss what they heard, especially at college, when having a good time seems foremost in many people's lives. But instead, this encounter changed my life.

Another life-changing event occurred to me in Florida. At the time, I was dating a few different girls, seeing them here and there—nothing serious. One girl's father was very ill, and she needed to return home to Virginia. She asked if I would consider going with her, as she was quite certain she would not be returning to college in Florida. While I was, of course, sympathetic, I had plans for life, which did not include settling down just yet or moving to Virginia. I was too young to make that sort of commitment.

She then asked me to do her a favor. She could not take her cocker spaniel on the flight home—it was too expensive. So, she asked me to take the dog. This seemed an easy-enough favor. I bid her goodbye—and I was suddenly the new owner of a rather disobedient dog, named Angie.

That afternoon, sun still out but cooler, I took the dog to the seventeenth floor of the condo where I lived and where my friends were hanging out. One of them turned around at the sight of me, a dog in my arms, and said, "Paul, do you understand when you own a dog, you have to walk the dog. And feed the dog." And I said, "Oh my God. Yeah, you're right. This poor little thing." It was not like living in a house where I could just open the door and let the dog into the yard.

Off I went to the elevator. Being in Florida, two elderly women were on the elevator as well, and I began chatting with them. The dog had been in my arms, but I put Angie on the floor and exchanged pleasantries with the women. All of a sudden, the doors slid open on the lobby, and the dog went eighty miles an hour out of the elevator, out of the lobby when someone opened the building's front door, and then out on the sand.

Sand is not easy to run on to begin with, let alone when you are chasing after a golden cocker spaniel who has no wish to be caught!

Ah, but the dog actually did me a favor. Because by the time I caught up to the runaway spaniel, there it sat between two beautiful girls in bikinis. Clever little beast! I walked over and said, "I'm so sorry. I apologize." One of them had beautiful blue eyes, and she and her friend were fussing over the dog, telling me how adorable it was.

I said to the one with blue eyes, "I know you don't know me, but my name is Paul. Would you want to go out with me?" She looked at me and said coyly, "Let me ask my friend. If she says yes, I'll go out with you." So, she turned around to another girl lying on a blanket, calmly reading a book. She said, "This guy wants me to go out with him. I don't know him. Do you think I should?"

Her blond-haired, fresh-faced friend glanced at me. "I think he looks like a bullshitter. I wouldn't go out with him if I were you."

I offered a little bow, and said, "OK. If your friend said that, I want to take my dog. I appreciate it, and it was a pleasure meeting you. I'm leaving."

I grabbed the dog, put a leash on the mischievous little pup, and started to walk away.

"Stop!" the first girl called after me. I turned back.

"Don't you want my number?" she asked.

I supposed I did! I took her number, and we ended up dating for about two months. One night, she told me that the two of us had been invited to a party on the Intracoastal. That night, we rang the doorbell of the party location, and the hostess was the beautiful girl who said I was a bullshitter. It was time for me to leave—and I hadn't even walked in.

She looked at me and said, "Don't be silly! Come on in. I was just joking with you."

All was forgiven, so I entered, and that party was amazing. The hostess knew how to make everyone feel comfortable and how to connect people. Then, party in full swing, music playing, all of a sudden, the hostess fell in the pool, and when she surfaced, she was gasping for air. I immediately dove in with my clothes on and brought her up and to the pool steps. I felt a little heroic! She thanked me and brought towels for the two of us, and we laughed. Then she said, "Do you want to leave this madness? Let's go to my boat. It's parked at the dock in the back." And we walked to the boat parked on the Intracoastal.

Once on the boat, she emphasized that she really was kidding that day on the beach. That night, on the water, under the stars sweeping across the horizon, we realized we liked each other—conversation with her was so easy, it was as if I had known her a long time. I broke up with my girlfriend in order to date Susan. And now we've been together for about fifty years.

I will not say our path to the altar was without a bump or two. I was a few years older than Susan, and her parents offered her flying lessons (a dream of hers) if she would only break up with me. I think they thought of me as a bit of a playboy, in that I dated around at first—and then she was too young to settle down. But Susan didn't waver. Since the bribe of flying lessons didn't work, they sent her off to college in Vermont—which is just about as far from Florida up the East Coast that one could get.

This was at a time when you called a person in their dorm on a pay phone in a hallway. My pals teased me relentlessly when she called me ("Lover Boy, it's for you!"), and when I called her, I had to wait while someone tracked her down in the dorm. While her parents (who ended up being very fond of me) may have hoped this would end our romance, after a year and a half, she insisted she loved me more than college in Vermont, and she returned to the Sunshine State and attended Florida Atlantic University, where she studied audiology.

By this time, I had dated models, professional tennis players, and women from different cultures and countries. I was fortunate to have the understanding that, in real life, you need to love someone, and that person needs to love you in return for *you* rather than being obsessed with your appearance or your money.

In Susan, there was an unconditional love for me. I knew that whether I ended up selling pizzas, or whether I became a billionaire, it didn't make any difference to her at all. I also realized how genuine and innocent she was, with this open heart and kindness. Despite the efforts to break us up, as time went on, the more I realized that she was the best possible woman for me.

Her father, a director at IBM, was transferred to Austin, Texas. She was there, far from me, and I was out one night with friends. I looked up at the night sky, at the stars I had shared with Susan, and realized my life was empty without her there. I could not fully explain it, but I was so alone without her.

At that moment, I knew if I did not ask her to marry me, I would regret it for the rest of my life. I called her to tell her I was coming to see her. I am not sure she had any idea how serious I was because when she was in Vermont, we had both dated other people. "Why are you coming to see me?" she asked over the phone.

"I just need to see you."

I flew to Austin—her father had bought an impressive home that had been President Lyndon B. Johnson's brother's house. The mansion had a magnificent terrace that looked out over the city. It was absolutely breathtaking. I don't know how happy her parents were to see me, but I was thrilled to see Susan.

After her parents went to sleep, the two of us stood on the terrace looking out on the lights of Austin—and the moon. It was one of those moments when you don't need to say anything at all, because it's so perfect, and to be sharing it with her made it even more so. I took her hand in mine and faced her. "You're not going to believe this, but I want to marry you."

Her eyes widened—and rather than saying yes right away, she asked me, "Are you serious?"

"I am very, very serious." And that was it. We were engaged. I had found my life partner who has gone on this crazy adventure of life with me—and what adventures we have had.

We told Susan's parents the next morning, and I had to head back to Florida to finish up school and graduate. She and her parents planned the most spectacular wedding back in the Sunshine State. Everything was flawless. And it was at a country club on the beach, a view of the beauty of the Atlantic Ocean.

The wedding was also rather hilarious. Her half of the guest list, in addition to her family, of course, was IBM people. They all had three-piece suits and not a hair out of place on their heads. Since this was before women were a more powerful part of the workforce, all these male executives had trophy wives in fancy cocktail dresses.

Then there was my half of the guest list. My friends were students, guys with long hair, girls in hippie fashions. However, it ended up being a great wedding—there is something about witnessing two people in love commit their lives to each other that brings out the joy in the people around them.

Meanwhile, I was a wreck. All my life—the stories I will share of incredible deals and projects, even massive setbacks, I always believed in myself. I am never nervous. But that night? I was.

The captain of the waiters, of the whole dining room operation, walked over to me and said, "Son, are you OK?" I confessed my nervousness, and he brought me a glass of Johnny Walker scotch. I was a beer guy, so I really did not have a tolerance for liquor. And when I say he brought me a *glass* of scotch, I do mean glass. I drank it down, felt the fire hit my gut, and found my nerves had settled. I went on to enjoy that incredible reception with my bride.

We then left for our honeymoon on Sanibel Island, a quiet and beautiful place on the West Coast of Florida, famous for its wide beaches and incredible varieties of shells. It's a sea glass and shell collector's paradise. (Sadly, it took a horrible hit from Hurricane Ian in 2022.)

I remember I scrimped and saved to be able to celebrate our first night with a bottle of Dom Perignon champagne. I popped the cork, feeling suave, and poured the golden bubbly into our two champagne flutes. I toasted my beautiful bride, and then we each took a sip. Susan immediately wrinkled up her nose. She *hated* the taste. So much for my grand gesture! She still does not like Dom Perignon.

At dinner the next night, I think the reality that we were husband and wife—'til death do us part—hit us. I looked at her, and I said, "I am not ever going to let you down." I have tried to honor that every day since then.

Now I was also thinking for two. I needed to make a decision on what I would do for my family—Susan was my family now, and we needed to build our life together. I intended to go to the graduate school.

Persians are similar to some other cultures, in which the expectation from your family is that you will be very educated. A doctorate would be the minimum. Being raised in that environment meant I would pursue my schooling further. I originally wanted to be an architect. I had one little problem—I hated math and was not very good at it. From my time in boarding school on through college, math remained my nemesis.

I knew I wanted to create things, though. I had gone to the library and researched graduate schools and programs, settling on urban planning. I knew it was a career with a degree of security—even though I also knew that since boyhood, I had the traits of an entrepreneur. First of all, an urban planner could work at any city in America. I still had dreams of the West Coast—dreams I inexplicably had even as a boy in Iran.

I also liked the way urban planning gives you an intimate look of what it takes to truly run a city. Think about it. You visit a city in your state—perhaps you live in one. How does clean drinking water come through the taps? How are parks planned? What developments will add something to the community? How are the streetlights kept on? Who programs the traffic lights?

I wanted to improve my ability to understand what the public sector was all about in America and in its infrastructure, who was calling the shots. We all know the saying, "You can't fight the city hall." I wanted to know exactly how to fight the city hall. I wanted to know what made cities tick.

To me, urban planning is the skeleton of the city, and the urban planner gets to look at every bone to see how it all fits together. Through my research, I discovered that Ball State University in Muncie, Indiana, had one of the best programs for urban planning in the United States. I applied and was accepted. Susan and I were off to Indiana, a land of soybeans and corn.

However, like my "welcome" to New York City in the middle of the night, my welcome to Indiana was not without its absurdity.

I had by now sold my Porsche and was again driving a Cadillac. An old one—because I was a broke student.

Now why did I do that? Because my life savings, all of my belongings, everything Susan and I owned had to be able to get it into a U-Haul trailer that we could drive from Florida to Ball State. As we were driving, I was telling Susan all of the things I planned to accomplish. Now, Susan is very practical. While she would listen, she also reminded me, "Paul, talk is cheap. You'll just have to show me when we get there."

Fair enough. As we drove, we continued talking, and in the middle of the freeway, that old beast of a car clunked and died. I opened the door, walked to the front of the car, opened the hood, and looked down at the engine. An engine I knew absolutely nothing about. I came back on the passenger side, and I told Susan that the car was gone. There was something wrong with the engine.

"Can you fix it?"

I walked back to the front of the car and stared down. I wouldn't know a carburetor if it fell on me from the sky. I walked back to the passenger-side window and shook my head. "No, I think we'll need to call a tow truck."

Of course, this was pre-cell phones, so we were going to have to wave down a passing vehicle. I leaned my arms on the window and continued to talk with her. All of a sudden, I started to feel terrible pain around my ankles. I had stepped directly on a colony of Florida's brutal fire ants. They were a half-inch thick on me and were climbing up my pant legs, viciously biting me along the way.

I hopped up and down, shouting some words I will not print in this book. Susan is shaking her head. "What is the matter with you?"

"Fire ants!" I shouted. Instead of sympathy, my crazy "ant dance" to get them off me sent her into spasms of laughter so hard that her eyes teared. I got most of them off me, and I opened the back door and jumped in to slide out of my pants and trade them for an ant-free pair.

Of course, at that moment, a police car zoomed up behind us, put on its blue lights—and I now had my pants down around my ankles. I had to explain to the policeman what happened, though he could see the ants going wild on the side of the road. He started laughing at my stupidity. Anyhow, he called us a tow truck to come and fix the car. Then we were off again. Such was my welcome to our new life.

Susan and I moved into graduate student housing. We were poor as the proverbial church mice—I had a little over $10,000 to last us the entire time of my schooling. I applied myself and focused—knowing it was *our* future on the line. I also had discovered a real passion. In fact, I was so passionate about urban planning that I earned straight As—except for one B+—the whole time I was in graduate school.

And about that B+. The professor had a heavy accent—and I had a difficult time understanding him. I struggled—as did most of my peers. However, I found the professor's textbooks—five of them. I bought them and read them all. (They were not very good.) Believe me, I did not have the spare dollars to be buying expensive texts, but I was hoping this might impress him. When I got the B+, I went to his office and hoped to show him how devoted I was to my studies—so much so I had read every word of his books. (I was probably the only one in the world aside from him and maybe his parents to have read them all.) I explained how every single other class I had taken at Ball State, I had earned an A.

He responded, "Well, nobody's perfect." The B+ remained and ruined my heretofore perfect GPA in graduate school.

While we were newlyweds there, Susan got a crash course in Persian culture. One of my uncles brought his son out to visit us in the winter—the young man was considering Ball State, and my uncle expected me to show my cousin around. In addition—as per our culture—my uncle was expecting us to not only let them stay with us but also to feed them, entertain them, and, in general, act as if we had nothing else to do but care for them.

My uncle was an important doctor—and he was scheduled to perform a complicated surgery. Unfortunately, Indiana is not noted for its balmy winter climate. A blizzard blew in and shut down the airport. My uncle was incensed that his flight was canceled—and wanted me to do something about it. More specifically, he wanted me to commandeer a helicopter to practically land in our parking lot and fly him off to his scheduled surgery. When I explained that I was a lowly graduate student and that *no one* would fly a helicopter in a blizzard, he was even more irate.

As I mentioned earlier, another expectation in Persian culture would be for me to obtain the most advanced degree in my field. However, once I earned my master's degree, I realized that a doctorate was not necessary for me, certainly at that moment. It would not advance my career—I needed to *start* my career. I wasn't planning to teach—the doctorate could wait. Of course, the irony is later on, I did lecture as a college instructor in California.

But, fresh master's degree in hand, an extraordinary thing occurred. A position had opened for a city manager in York Town, Indiana. One of my professors recommended me for the job.

"You are insane," I told my professor. "I've never worked in the field of urban planning. I've never been a city manager!"

I also had a dual degree—in public administration as well as urban studies—which made me a bit unique. I just had no work experience. However, just as the Mon Pères in the boarding school, and the professor in Florida, this man had faith in me. "I believe in you, Paul. You were one of my best students ever. You have studied hard. You can do this."

I was less sure. Though I had read everything I could on urban planning and city management, it was all hypothetical. However, I received an invitation to interview. Out of fifty or sixty candidates, shockingly, I was the one they offered the job to. When I look back at it, I know I did extraordinarily well in the interview. Why? Because I believed I had no chance to get the job, so it was all good "practice" for whatever job I would eventually get. I also had a longing to go to California, so staying in Indiana wasn't part of my big life plan. During the interview, I answered everything very honestly (as you'll recall, I do believe honesty is the best policy). "Have you done this before?" "No, sir. I haven't. But I'm an excellent student because I understand city management and urban planning." Mind you, if you do not know, in terms of my field, city *planning* is a different beast than city *management.*

People respond to honesty, though, I think. Honesty is how I've chosen to live my life. I'll add that through all this time, Susan was my partner in every sense of the word. We were a team. With Susan, I could 100 percent be myself. Do you know, to this day, I see people who pretend with their own spouses or partners? They might live in a mansion on a cliffside above Los Angeles, but they are mortgaged over their heads—and no one knows. Not their spouses, not their close friends. I've always told Susan everything. How else can we be a team to achieve our goals and the life we want to live?

In any case, the honesty paid off, and York Town took a chance on me.

I was a kid! I had no experience. All I can say is that I had no clue. But I was soon to get a crash course in running a city. On my first day, I showed up and was escorted to my office. For a near twenty-five-year-old kid, fresh out of graduate school, it was like winning the lottery. The office was elegant with a magnificent, polished desk, bookshelves, and a view out the window. I had an American flag on one side of the door on a brass flagpole and the state flag on the other side. It was surreal.

Then as I sat down in my leather desk chair, in walked an attractive young woman in a miniskirt (the fashion of the times).

"How do you take your coffee, Mr. Owhadi?" she asked, after introducing herself to me as my secretary.

I had just come from a college environment. Now, here I had my own office (with a bouquet of fresh flowers on the desk by way of welcome) and my own secretary—and no idea just yet all that was involved in being a city manager. It was sink or swim.

I swam.

One thing I have always believed is that you should surround yourself with people smarter than yourself—with the very best people. You should also never be afraid to ask questions. So, I picked other people's brains. I constantly approached people, anybody I would see who had something to contribute to the running of York Town.

I was the youngest city manager in the state now. I am not sure Susan even thought this was real. When I had first told her I was interviewing, she was very much like, "I'll believe it when I see it."

One of the secrets of my success is a gift that not everyone would think of as a gift. I have attention deficit disorder (ADD). Because of this specialness, I can juggle many processes and tasks and ideas at once. When I'm at a restaurant having dinner with someone, I can hear the conversation at the tables around me simultaneously. You can't inject this into someone. It has to be natural, has to come forward. You have to be blessed. Some, as I said, might not think of it that way, but I do. And this talent enabled me to leap into the deep end of city management and not sink.

Now, on that first day as city manager, I was dressed in a three-piece blue suit with a burgundy tie. I liked being well-dressed. My secretary had come in and asked about getting me coffee. I told her I could get my own, but she insisted. When she brought the coffee back, she said, "The police chief would like to see you." Although I had studied what municipalities were all about, for some odd reason, because I was so young, I didn't realize that the police chief worked for me now.

"Veronica, you can tell him I'm settling in, and go ahead and set up a meeting when it's convenient for him."

"No, no, sir, you don't understand. He's in the waiting room. He wants to see you now."

She put the coffee in front of me, and I leaned back in my comfortable leather chair, shut my eyes for a second to ground myself, and thought, "Right, he works for me."

I nodded, and she left and returned with, in my twentysomething mind, this old man. Of course, now I realize he was probably in his forties. Isn't it funny how our definition of "old" changes?

He came in, dressed in a blue uniform, shook my hand, and said, "Nice to meet you, sir."

I almost looked around the room. Who was he calling "sir"?

He sat opposite to me and said, "I came over to introduce myself and to ask you your policies and what would you like me to concentrate on."

Since until five minutes before that, I had no idea I was even to have anything to do with the police department. I simply said, "Carry on as you are."

That seemed like safe advice for the moment.

Just like being a student in school, and a student of life, and of cultures and people, I was a student of my own field. I worked tirelessly—I always give 100 percent. I learned all that I could about York Town. I mastered the city manager job, and I got involved with development, zoning, planning, all of the public works. You can think of a city manager as a chief executive officer, only it's a public corporation, not a private one.

As the city manager, I was in charge of all the departments—police, fire planning, public works. When I would hold a meeting in our conference room, I would have most department heads. They all would report to me what was going on in their department. I was in charge of hiring and firing of all the employees. My job was to run the city and be accountable to the city council. I would present reports to the city council during their public meetings. I would basically present to them the affairs of the city. If they liked the way things were going, they would take credit for it, of course, because it's politics. If they didn't like the way it was going, they blamed the city manager, a.k.a., *me.*

How did I manage this all at such a young age? Number one, I was street-smart. If you are sheltered, you are not savvy enough—because in such a high-pressure job, you need to be fearless. I really had no fear of failure. Failure was not in my vocabulary. I would say to myself, *Hey, if I don't understand it, I'll fix it. If I make a mistake, that is how I will learn.*

I also surrounded myself with loyal employees who understood that I needed to learn, but yet, they respected me as their boss—and I treated them with respect. All these years later, with deals worth many tens of millions of dollars, with thirty, forty, fifty companies at any given time, guess what? That thinking still holds. With all my companies, I hire the very best people I can find, I compensate them fairly, and I let them run things and report to me. I know that your team is a vital part of your success.

I was there for several years and learned all I could. But I had more to learn—I wanted to take on new challenges, new cities.

Someplace new came calling. If you have ever been to the Cincinnati airport—even if just to change planes—you have been to my next city. Except it's not Cincinnati at all. That airport is in Kentucky! And that was the next stop on my journey.

Reflection Questions

1. Have you ever been in a job where you were in over your head? How did you handle it? What did you learn from it?

2. I was fortunate to find my soulmate and cocaptain early in my life. Who are your cocaptains? Who are the members of your personal "team"?

3. Have you found your passion in work?

4. How do you handle fear?

5. Once again, I had a mentor or someone who believed in me to push me. What have the mentors in your life done for you? How have they pushed you to better yourself or to stretch your talents? Have you paid that forward?

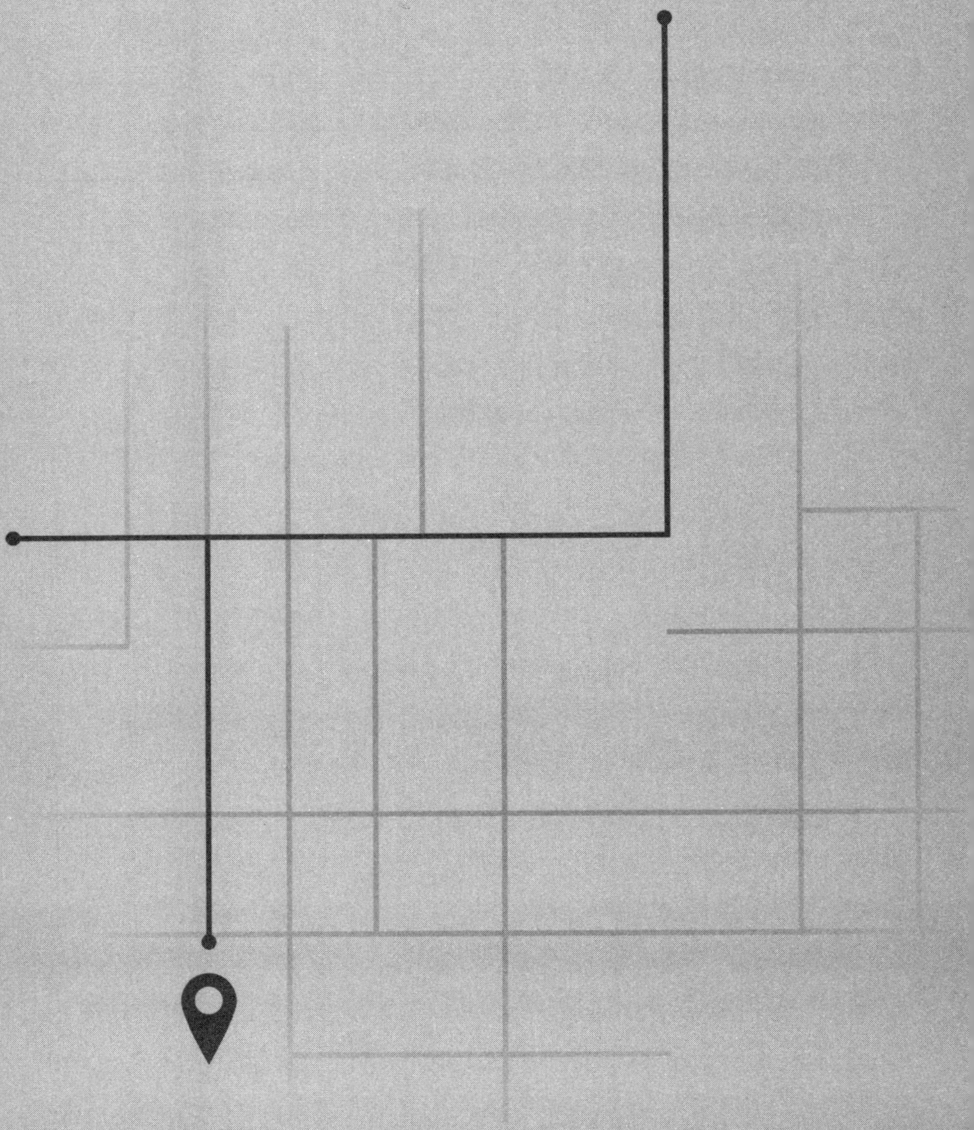

CHAPTER FIVE

Going Places

Congratulations! Today is your day. You're off to Great Places! You're off and away!

—DR. SEUSS, OH, THE PLACES YOU'LL GO!

Susan and I packed up for Kentucky—only now there were two and a half of us. Susan was expecting. We were on our way to a bigger city and a whole new area.

This time, starting out, I at least knew what a city manager *did.* I had cut my teeth in Indiana, and now I was managing Ludlow, which is a riverfront city near Covington and Cincinnati.

The mayor, Peter Klosterman, was in his eighties and a bit of a character with salty language, suspenders, and a bow tie—sort of out of central casting of an old Kentuckian. I remember sitting in his grand office, a fireplace against the wall, dark, clubby wood, and wingback chairs, and asking him, "Mr. Mayor, what would you like me to do among the first assignments?"

He leaned back in his enormous leather chair and drawled, “Do whatever you want to do. But if I were you, I would clean up some of these goddamn topless bars.”

This was around 1978. The bars made one area of the city seem extremely rough. At night, prostitutes openly strolled the streets as cars and trucks passed through. Bar fights regularly ended up spilling out onto the sidewalks, and everything was rundown and dirty. Yet I had a vision of what it *could* be. That was my gift as a city manager—being able to “see” what a city could become.

I said to the mayor, “If you close all of these topless bars, you will begin to develop the environment that you are looking for. You want a family environment, you’re right near the water—always a plus. Think if that area could be developed. This city has a lot of potential. And if people see all of these hookers hanging around outside the bars, along with the johns and no doubt drugs and pimps, this will *never* be a place couples will go to for a nice evening out; no matter what restaurants you open, what the water view is, families will not come.”

Of course, I did not quite understand just *how* loyal fans of strip clubs can be. In this town, that was actually a bit of an understatement. We ended up closing four or five bars, the worst, seediest offenders. All of a sudden, at the next city council meeting, about two hundred unruly customers, bouncers, and rough-looking patrons came to the city hall, along with a few of the strippers in street clothes, and they demanded my resignation. The scene was ugly with a tremendous negative energy filling the room. All that was missing were pitchforks.

One of biggest, roughest guys with some neo-Nazi tattoos stood and in a booming voice, shouted at me, “Why don’t you go back where you came from?” because the crowd knew I was of Persian descent.

The police chief, a large man with a protruding beer gut and a doughy face, was sitting next to me at the council meeting. Since he worked for me, I leaned over and whispered, "You have three seconds to get these people out. Otherwise, you leave both your badge and your gun with me."

I was now even more confident than that young graduate with a fresh degree in Indiana. I knew if I did not make a show of strength, I was essentially finished as city manager. This is one of the more important life and business lessons I mastered. *Read the room.*

I read it and knew I needed to make an impression.

The police chief also read the room and my face, which showed I was deadly serious. Meanwhile the room was electric with volatile people. All it needed was a spark. At any moment, I expected fists to fly. The chief rose and lumbered to the middle of the council chamber and shouted, "You've got three seconds to evacuate!"

And everyone left, a few of them muttering. But the troublemakers were all gone in under five minutes.

I found out later that the police chief was one of the top clients of all of these strip club bars. In running a city, there are always details like that hidden beneath the surface, behind closed doors, open secrets or whispered gossip. He would go to that district at night and get free booze (he was fond of cheap bourbon) and free lap dances. So, it was not a pleasant thing for him to shut them down—and no doubt his "pals" running these places were quite angry.

But the decision to shut those businesses was the best one I could have made. In short order, things started to turn around for my new city. Currently, it is one of the finest cities in Kentucky, a bedroom community to the city of Cincinnati. There are wonderful restaurants, waterfront development, good schools, and parks—an ideal place to raise a family. That town really grew, but it had to start with making it safe and clean. This is an essential lesson for any city planner or developer.

I had another motivation for making the city as wonderful as I could. Susan and I were soon to be parents.

I was so excited about being a father. This was at the beginning of Lamaze classes being taught to nearly all parents (whereas, just a generation before, men were rarely even in the delivery room). After a long day at City Hall, at five-thirty on the appointed evenings, I would go in a three-piece suit to this class where we were going to breathe together and learn how to bring a baby into the world. Everybody else was in their T-shirts and sweats—I was the one with the fancy suit.

Then the day actually came—time for our baby to be born. We rushed to the hospital, which had a brand-new state-of-the-art maternity wing. In class, of course, they had taught us how to breathe, how to hold the pregnant woman's hand, and how to use a pillow to get her comfortable. However, there was not a Lamaze pillow to be found anywhere in the hospital.

I am of the opinion, whatever a woman in labor wants, *get it.* Quickly!

The labor and delivery nurses, eyes wide, kept apologizing. "I'm so sorry, sir, this wing is so new. We don't have a pillow for her. We've sent for one."

By now, poor Susan was well into labor. It is difficult to see the person you love most in the world in pain. I tried to calm her, to be a soothing presence. I'll never forget how she grabbed my hand so hard that she almost cut my flesh. I think she said a few choice words about Lamaze. (And far be it for any *man* to complain about a thing during labor and delivery as the woman is the one having a child!) But before we knew it (well, I am sure for Susan, she knew it!), Michelle was born, and from the moment that I saw the face of this beautiful angel, my life changed.

There really are places in the heart you don't even know exist until you love a child.
—ANNE LAMOTT

Though I am sure many parents are reading this book, it remains true that there is no way to describe the moment when you become a parent to someone who has not had the same experience. You can speak of a love that surpasses all understanding, but it's still impossible to convey. When that cry is first heard, so many of the anxieties of the last nine months—Will the baby be born healthy? Will everything go all right?—melt into tears of joy. They brought our perfect little daughter, all wrapped in a soft pink, blue, and white blanket and a tiny cap, to Susan and me. I stood there, and I thanked God in that moment. I also knew I would be working harder than ever to provide a life of opportunity and happiness for my little family.

Susan and I embarked on life as parents. Meanwhile, at my job, the mayor certainly made my life interesting. He was very charismatic—a gray-haired man with a twinkle in his blue eyes. One day, I remember he came into my office, and he had a pouty face—not in a mean way but a little silly. He shut the door behind him and said, "Paul, Paul ... I need to talk to you."

I asked if he wanted some coffee, but he shook his head. "Nope. I want to talk to you."

Now this seemed serious.

"Write this down." He rattled off an address at an intersection. "I want you to go ahead and fix the goddamn effing light pole, the light at that intersection. It's out."

"OK," I said. This certainly was odd. And not the sort of thing a typical mayor concerned himself with.

"It's dark at night over there. I want you to put everything aside. And I want you to go ahead and have this fixed today."

I tried to hide my surprise and replied, "Well, Pete, we can't do that. You know what I mean? I have to put in a work order. But I can certainly make it a priority."

"Paul, you don't understand—I want this fixed today."

The mayor wasn't budging. So, I pulled every trick in my book to be able to get people shifted and a work crew at the intersection. I still, frankly, found it puzzling.

The work crew reported back to me that they had fixed the light, so I called the mayor. "Pete, you know, I like you a lot." (It's always good to make the mayor happy.) "And I took care of it for you. The light is fixed."

"OK," he said and then hung up after a fast goodbye.

This was eccentric—even for him. The next day, he again came to my office. This time, he was jovial, beaming. When I asked if he wanted coffee, he smiled and said, "Gladly."

My secretary brought in coffee and then left, closing the door. The mayor grinned. "I got even with her."

Now I was thoroughly confused. "With whom?"

"Remember when I said I needed you to fix the light. That's because the lady who lived on that corner has called my house at three in the morning to complain about it being out. Middle of the night! Waking me out of a dead sleep."

"I see," I said, only I didn't see at all.

"Well, I called her last night at two-thirty in the morning. I said, 'Madam, the light is fixed.'"

Yes, my time in the town was certainly with unique challenges. Another lesson: You never know what any day will hold. The key is to always adapt to any situation—and any "character" like the mayor.

And adapt I did. My work was very successful.

In fact, in December 1979, Governor John Y. Brown Jr. was sworn in as governor of Kentucky. At the time, he was married to Phyllis George, a sportscaster and former Miss America. Brown was famous for buying Kentucky Fried Chicken off "Colonel Sanders." He changed it to more of a fast-food business and made it a massive success. (He later partnered with Kenny Rodgers' Roasters chain as well.) Brown was elected at a time when Kentucky was in an economic downturn. Oil prices had skyrocketed; inflation hit 11 percent. The United States was entering a recession (the following year inflation hit 20 percent). Brown ran on a platform in which he would approach running the state more like a business. Having a glamorous wife also helped parlay him to the governor's mansion. They were a formidable political couple.

The governor's office contacted me during his term, and his spokesperson said that Governor Brown had heard of what my team and I had done in the city. Brown indicated through his staff that he would like to come to my town and recognize the changes.

The day was so memorable. The beautiful Phyllis George and her governor-husband flew down with their entourage. At a ceremony, he commissioned me as an honorary Kentucky colonel. Now, at the time, I didn't know what the heck that was, but they informed me it is an honor bestowed only by the governor of Kentucky. It is highest honor awarded by the Commonwealth of Kentucky, and colonels are considered ambassadors of goodwill and are honored for their contributions to the community, state, or nation.

I still have the gold-embossed certificate. I guess you can call me Colonel Paul. Susan was holding Michelle, just an infant, and Phyllis George was standing next to Susan. She leaned over and whispered in Susan's ear. I could hear what she said because I was standing next to her and the governor was next to me. Phyllis George's secret was she was pregnant, just very early on and not ready to tell many people yet. Every time I watch CNN and see the anchor Pamela Brown, who happens to be Phyllis George's daughter, it reminds me of that moment.

They spent the whole day in our city, making appearances, seeing the positive changes we were implementing. The whole day and the honor was a wonderful thing for the community, for me personally, and for what I was trying to achieve in making our town a family-friendly, business-friendly location. I felt deep pride in watching and being an essential part of the transformation. The very things that drew me to urban planning—being able to put my mark on a city—were coming to fruition.

But despite all these terrific things, I knew in my work life, I needed to move on. First, I was bored. Boredom will be the kiss of death in life. And in business and a career. You become stagnant. You cease growing. I had my eyes on still bigger adventures—I would never be content to be still. I still am not. The idea of retiring is completely foreign to me.

I had a master plan in my mind. All my life, I felt the allure of California. Even as a little boy in Shiraz, I was certain I would one day live in California. Every time I saw a photo of Carmel in a magazine, I pictured myself there. California was a land of opportunity—a valuable state with so much to offer in terms of resources, climate, and natural beauty. The beauty of the pounding Pacific, the majestic Sierra Nevada mountains, the Pacific Coast Highway, San Francisco's beautiful Victorian homes on the Bay, fruit trees, and the glitz of Los Angeles and Hollywood. So, I basically opened up a book of maps and looked at California and the cities and areas near Carmel. I pinpointed on Fresno as well. I told Susan, "I'm going to apply out there, and the first job I get, I'm going to take it. I don't care where it is, as long as it is on the West Coast. I'm going to go there. I'm going to work for a year. And then I am going to make the leap from the public to the private sector."

In my work as a city manager, I made a nice living, I had job security (every city needs a manager!), but I was on a fixed salary. Meanwhile, I saw the developers and others I was working with arrive on private jets, making many multiples of millions of dollars. I knew that their visions were not any greater or wiser than my own. I was certain in the private sector I could do more—follow my own path. I envisioned being an entrepreneur—it had always been my long-term plan. As a city manager, though many people reported to me, I was also, essentially, working for a whole city—many bosses. It was time to be my own boss.

I was never about the money. I saw money as a vehicle, a catalyst to be able to do nice things for the people I love. It's not the end goal. What you can do *with* it—including travel, philanthropy, making life easier for your elderly parents, being able to afford a comfortable life—that is what money is for, not an end unto itself. My father used to say, "I cannot feast on a lavish meal while knowing a neighbor is hungry." Money helped me do positive things for my family—and my community.

Susan is a remarkable partner, something part of so much of my and our story. Her response was, "Whatever you want, I'll back you up. But remember, we have a baby now."

If anything, having a child (we eventually had three: Michelle, Chris, and Jennifer, all bright and successful in their own right) made me *more* determined to forge my own pathway. But I will never underestimate receiving support from the people whom I needed the most. Susan believed in me—and that made me all the more determined.

Our next stop was California. Though how I got there was, as usual, a story.

I had received a call from Mendota, California, a city in Fresno County. They flew me out, but we had already had preliminary discussions, and so it looked very favorable for me. However, when I landed and got my rental car, I discovered this "city" was actual in the center of flat, agricultural lands that stretched for hundreds upon hundreds of miles. Fresno County is considered the agricultural capital of the United States. Farmers there grow almonds, grapes, garlic, tomatoes, and more, as well as produce milk, poultry, cattle, and cantaloupes.

I think the city council viewed my trip there as a formality—after all, they had paid for me to fly out there and for my rental car and hotel room. But I pulled over to a payphone at a gas station (yes, it was the days before cell phones) and called Susan.

"I've been driving for an hour, and it's just flat land for miles on miles. I don't think I can move here, Susan. I don't think I can take the job."

This certainly was not the "California Dreamin'" I'd been picturing.

Susan replied, "But I thought you said you would take whatever job came along just to get us out to the West Coast."

Ah, don't we all hate it when the people we love remind us of what we said?

I knew she was right, but the town had only about fifteen thousand people, and I just could not get past how rural it was. There was very little going for it in my mind. To the mayor and the city council's shock, I turned down the job. I apologized profusely. "I know you have flown me all the way out here from Kentucky, but I just don't think this is for me. It was not what I expected."

When I returned home early, Susan was surprised. I said, "Honey, I love you very, very much, but this is not my cup of tea. You know, I don't want to go out there."

Susan, always my partner in all things in life, told me it was OK, but I also felt torn. We had established deadlines—"We'll be in California by such and such a date," and "I'll look for a job in the private sector within a year to eighteen months." I did not like breaking my commitment to our plan.

Then the phone rang as we were sitting talking about our future plans. The caller was the city manager of Fresno, who was the head of the committee I had just interviewed with. "Paul, I know you're disappointed. Maybe I should have prepared you a little more for what it's like out here." This was before you could log onto Google Earth or Wikipedia and learn more about a place. The man continued, "You told me on day one when we spoke that your goal was to come to California, and the committee really wants you badly. And they're going to double your salary."

This put an interesting spin on things. So, I decided to try to sweeten the deal a little. "If that's the case, I want my BMW shipped there."

As the conversation went on, I just kept adding to my list of requests. "And I really don't think my wife would be very happy living someplace so rural. She needs a metropolitan area. So I would commute back and forth—and so I'd like a city car to be able to do that."

I kept putting out additional requests—secretly hoping, I think, that I could say to Susan, "They didn't meet my contract demands."

But everything I asked for, they gave me, until there was really no way to tell them no. So, I rented a house in the city of Fresno, whose population was around about 200,000 at the time—a city big enough for Susan and the baby to make a life. I commuted about forty-five minutes each way. But the life of a city manager is not nine to five by any stretch. Sometimes committee meetings went past midnight. I saw very little of Susan, and she had to soldier on, in some ways almost a single mom.

I was exhausted all the time. The town was on the verge of bankruptcy. Most of the population were poorer agricultural workers. The town had wanted me so badly because they had seen my history—and they knew I could transform the place. I'm proud to say I changed the course and fortunes of that little town.

The municipality was in the red when I arrived and, through my efforts, was brought to solvency. I was able to subsidize the cost of construction of major capital improvements with federal and state grants. I implemented multiple redevelopment projects throughout the city, but it was hard work. Remember how the mayor of the Kentucky town told me to close the strip clubs? The mayor of this town wanted to *add* them for tax money. But I stuck to my plans—eventually earning the accolades of Congressman Tony Coelho, who saw the changes were making life in my city better.

I looked at it this way: when you manage cities for years, you learn the craft, and it's like being a pilot. You get a certain number of flying hours under your belt—and all of a sudden, you are a seasoned pilot. Cities fail and go bankrupt for a number of reasons. The city council, for example, is very important. If they have poor leadership, it holds a city back. If the city manager's not savvy or doesn't care, everything just basically sits idle and goes nowhere. I was a very aggressive and proactive city manager. I formed the redevelopment agency in order to generate the revenues that the city was not otherwise entitled to receive. The redevelopment agency attracted developers and investors and ultimately played a very important part in my fate and path.

One story, which shows what a city manager is sometimes up against, is I had magnificent trees installed leading into the town. We had a large welcome sign. We had landscaping done. I wanted anyone driving down that boring rural highway to come into our town and feel that it was a wonderful place.

The mature trees were all planted, and they cost thousands of dollars.

And overnight, they were all stolen.

Huge trees. Gone. Holes in the ground where they had been planted. No doubt the thieves planned to resell them.

But this is one of the things you encounter when you try to evolve and change a place. How does a city manager combat that? For one thing, pride. Involving the town in the changes, involving as many people as possible, will help to bring people together in the spirit of improving a city.

Improving a city is about commitment. And I was always deeply committed to what I did. To me, any job worth doing is worth doing *exceptionally.* One night, I was commuting back to Fresno late at night with a horrible fog (one of the unfortunate things about my commute—often foggy), using one of the city's unmarked police cars. Suddenly, a young couple in a car did not see the stop sign at the intersection—and they T-boned me at sixty miles per hour. I broke the windshield with my head (before the day of airbags, of course).

The man climbed from the wreck of his car and started screaming at me that I had killed his wife. I felt an undercurrent of violence and fury from him (even though the accident was his fault).

When he saw and heard the police radio in my car, he backed off. Thank God, she was not killed—she had a broken leg and cuts and bruises. I was able to radio for help, and I made it home, finally, with a police ride, sometime past three o'clock.

The next day, I took Susan's car, and my bandaged-up head, and was back at work. It would never dawn on me to take a sick day. When it comes to my own employees and family members, I do believe you should take care and take a sick day if you need. But it's just not how I am wired. I think entrepreneurs are born that way.

I applied that entrepreneurial mindset to my city. I took the redevelopment agency I had for my own city—and then called four or five other cities and asked if they would like to participate in a joint venture in order to attract industries beneficial to each city. Combine several small cities, and there is more power than a single small city on their own.

But what I was doing with redevelopment and bonds and municipal projects was attracting attention. I was getting press coverage. Two kinds.

Sometimes I say I must have lived on the West Coast in another life. Something about it felt like "home" even before I arrived. After our relocation, one additional very special part of my journey happened. I was settled into my job as a city manager. I was living in the land of sunshine and citrus. One of my best friends was a special agent in the FBI. We were having dinner one night, and I told him that I had been in the United States a long time with a permanent residency. I wanted to finalize my citizenship. I'd been so busy with my work that I had not made it a priority. However, I did not want to be sworn in with a large class in public, as usually happens, because of the revolution back in Iran.

It sounds so strange. I had left Iran as an adolescent. But some of the newspapers there printed articles with my face, name, and the fact that I was working for the U.S. government. I knew there was no chance I could ever go home to the country of my birth. Thankfully, my parents had also been able to come to the United States. The upheaval, however, in Iran, meant my work in the United States, my life *here*, would be very much misunderstood *there*.

My dear friend, Tom, the FBI special agent, approached a federal judge—Judge Edward Dean Price. He told him, "My friend, Paul, a city manager in Fresno County, wants to be sworn in as a U.S. citizen but in private."

The judge agreed. I went to his chamber, and it was as if my life came full circle. He was smoking his pipe, and it smelled so good, was so evocative. It reminded me of the American general whom I had met back in Iran as a young boy—the one I so eagerly practiced my English with. Sometimes life sends you those little reminders—of how far you have come, of your life so far. It was as if all the events of my life, from that little boy practicing his English to that moment in the judge's chambers, flashed in front of me.

And there, in his thick-carpeted office, in his black robes, with the scent of cherry, tobacco, cinnamon, and patchouli, the judge intoned, "Mr. Owhadi, it's my honor to do this for you." Thus, I was sworn in as a U.S. citizen, in 1980—a most special day in my life, other than the birth of my children. In my mind, it was a quintessential American moment.

I was incredibly aware of the true *freedom* I had—and that another path, another choice at any crossroads, and I might not have breathed freely in America. I would have been in Iran, fearful for my safety and that of my family.

However, this press coverage I was receiving, which had forced me to declare my oath of allegiance to the United States in a judge's chambers, was also about to bring me a good kind of attention—and introduce me to a man who would change my life.

One thing to remember in any story of success: when opportunity knocks, answer the door!

Reflection Questions

1. Have you ever had a dream you could not explain but you knew you had to pursue it?

2. What does reading the room mean to you? Why is it so important in business?

3. Can you name a time when personal readiness met opportunity in your life?

4. Have you ever made a huge leap of faith in business?

5. Do you listen to your gut? Or second-guess yourself? Why or why not?

CHAPTER SIX
Opportunity Knocks

If opportunity doesn't knock, build a door.
—MILTON BERLE

The successes I was having (and the opportunity that was soon to come) would be meaningless without my family. The philosopher Frederick Nietzsche famously wrote, "He who has a why can endure any how." Susan and our children were and remain my why.

In addition, Susan and I always chose "experiences" for our kids over material things. We did all we could to save money in order to travel—and we brought our kids along. I wanted them to see more than just America, because my own experiences around the world had brought me unique perspectives about life. Somehow, I think travel makes the world a little smaller, more intimate.

Meanwhile, in California, my family was flourishing. When we had moved, we decided it was time to buy a home at last. Our first house was in the city of Fresno, where Susan was carving out a life, and we were living at the time, with me commuting back and forth.

Interest rates at the time were 18 percent. I know that's an astounding number.

But we felt very lucky when we got a lower variable rate, and we found a house and negotiated to buy it at $105,000. We fell in love with the house, but it was going to be a stretch. We put down the least amount we could. And when it came time to close, we were short $280 in escrow. That may not sound like much, but at the time it could have been a million. I had no idea where to get the extra money. Even if I had, I would have been loath to borrow from someone.

Susan, however, can play music beautifully—both the piano and the flute. Her parents had bought her a beautiful silver flute, which she treasured. Susan, always my partner, resolved to sell it so that we could buy the house. We ended up selling it for $310. So, with $30 to spare, we bought our house and took the keys to start a new chapter of our lives.

Our house had an in-ground pool, and that first night, I turned its light on. The master bedroom faced it, with a French door where we could look out at it. Susan, exhausted from the move, fell sound asleep. But I stayed up in the silence of our new house until about two in the morning. I first went to check on my children—by now my second child had been born. After watching them sleep for a moment, I went back and stood at the French doors of my bedroom and stared at the yard that was now ours. And the bank's, of course. Every so often, I would rouse Susan and say, "Susan, this is our house. Look at this. We have a swimming pool. We have a backyard. The kids can play back there and grow up here."

She would smile sleepily and say, "I know, I'm so happy. It's wonderful."

Sometimes she would join me and stare at the pool until she fell asleep again. And then I'd wake her up a half hour later to marvel all over again.

It's at moments like that when you pause at those monumental events in your life when you know you have crossed some kind of Rubicon, that you consider where you came from and how far you've traveled. From the little boy in a boarding school far from home, to the young man on his own in London, to landing in New York City with just a few hundred dollars, to all my adventures along the way to meeting my wife in Florida, to graduate school, and then the launch of my career, they had all brought me to the distant land of California to a life I could not fully have dreamed of. A life of freedom in the United States.

It seemed like a dream.

Meanwhile, in my career, I was not a magician, but the city I managed thought I was indeed doing magical things—pulling proverbial rabbits out of hats. Only with my vision of what we could be, not sleight of hand.

My new opportunity came as a direct result of the work I was doing and the attention I was attracting. I formed a redevelopment agency, and because my city had blight, we had the option of "capturing" 100 percent of our tax dollars for redevelopment because of how California (at the time) was handling improvements in blighted areas.

Suddenly, we had millions of tax dollars instead of apportioning some of it to the state. In addition, I knew how to take that money and issue tax anticipation notes. The revenues facilitated the ambitious projects I had planned. In essence, those tax anticipation notes let the development world know our municipality was open for development—open for business!

In the meantime, so I would not lose tens of thousands of dollars of trees again, I was involving the people of the municipality more and more. I reached out to them across all sectors. By involving them, I wanted them to take pride of ownership in the place where they lived.

I formed the redevelopment agency for my city and then assisted several other nearby cities with the formation of their own redevelopment agencies. We shared some of the same problems—and the same goals. To make our cities successful, by forming these agencies, we were able to band together on select projects and negotiate together as a bloc.

For example, cable television did not really exist—and certainly not in our rural area. TV in our town was about six channels—not all of which came in clearly. I brought all these five cities under one umbrella. And that gave me negotiating power with the emerging cable companies. As the chairman of the committee, I was like the CEO. It was time to wheel and deal, as they say. I negotiated with a cable company from Los Angeles that ordinarily would never have considered coming to the flatlands of agricultural California. But with five other cities, we were suddenly attractive. Bringing in cable was a huge and appreciated change for the people of our municipalities.

At the time I was considered a radical guy in my approach. I was a city manager. These kinds of projects, especially out there, were unheard of. But I didn't care what people thought. The Latin phrase "fortune favors the bold" applied to me. I would do what I envisioned because I was ready to leave for the private sector if the right opportunity appeared. My ambition was not to be a city manager of Los Angeles or a bigger city. I was not there to play it safe. This job was a stopping point on the way to making the leap to the next step in my career. Therefore, I was unafraid to make waves.

Sometimes the degree of your success or failure hinges on thinking outside the box and being willing to walk a path that has not been established yet. So, it was my ambitious plans for the municipality and the way I was handling redevelopment that attracted the attention of a giant in the construction and development world, Sheldon Pollack. His was an ingenious company—everything was in-house. Architects, lawyers, engineers, anything needed for large-scale construction projects. It was one of the most successful development companies in the United States.

Several engineers representing the Pollack Corporation and Pacific Architects and Engineers (an international engineering firm known as PAE) visited the city in search of an ideal site for the construction of a twenty-five-megawatt co-generation facility under a joint venture agreement by and between their respective entities and the redevelopment agency. The most logical place to build in California would be at the center of an agricultural area because of the availability of agricultural and biowaste from farming. The Pollock Corporation did their due diligence and did thorough research into Fresno County (and, as it turned out, me). Then his company came, and they told us that they wanted to invest a hundred million minimum in our town. When this happens, it's a bit like "courting"—who is going to do what to sweeten the deal? Since they would generate revenue and taxes for my city from their project, they wanted to see what we could provide for them through the available tax anticipation notes and revenues from the redevelopment agency. We were attracting businesses that wouldn't have considered our municipality before I arrived. We were a bit like Cinderella at the ball.

A few days after meeting these gentlemen from the development group, my secretary walked in my office and said that Sheldon Pollack's people were on the line. I hadn't met him yet—and Sheldon apparently wanted to speak with me. I told her to schedule a call. But as it turned out, he wanted a face-to-face meeting. So, I told her to make arrangements for the following week. But again, as it turned out, he wanted something more. To meet *now.* And he intended to land at a nearby airport catering mostly to private planes in Fresno. He was a man with exceptional business instincts who liked to size up who he might be working with. He wanted a real-life connection, not to chat on the telephone.

A power plant would be a significant asset for Fresno County, so I did what any good city manager would—I hopped in my city car and headed to the airport. I waited by a metal hangar on the private side of the airport, which was surrounded by scrubby weeds on the outside of the fence. Suddenly this beautiful, sleek, *gleaming* Cessna rolled down the runway and came to a stop. The door opened, and a staircase descended dramatically. Out came a very handsome man about six-foot-three with telegenic silver hair and intense blue eyes. His suit looked to be Hugo Boss, probably several thousand dollars, tailored to him perfectly. Expensive Italian loafers. Discreet diamond cufflinks. Shirt perfectly starched. He was just immaculately well-dressed and striking.

He shook my hand, and we introduced ourselves to each other. "Take me to your best restaurant," he said.

I had to break it to him that the "best" around the airport was a pizza joint.

"Is that really the best you can do?"

"I'm afraid so, sir, unless you want to drive thirty or forty-five minutes away—and most of those places require a reservation."

So, the pizza place it was. I was immensely curious as to both this man and this power plant he wanted to build. This was before the internet was so ubiquitous, so it wasn't as if I could Google and do a deep dive as to him and his company.

We went to the local Italian place, a place with Chianti-bottle candles on the tables, red ruffled curtains on the mirror, and linoleum floors. He told me that he had heard of me through his head engineer, as well as the League of California Cities—most of the 450-plus cities in California were members of the association. I had done an interesting downtown development project in a very innovative way with tax-exempt bonds and some intelligent, new ways of financing it successfully.

Sheldon looked at me over the red-checkered tablecloth. "We're planning to build a power plant in your town. I wanted to check it out, make sure your redevelopment agency is fully solvent."

I assured him we were. I told him about some of our other projects and some of my plans for the city. Two hours went by as if it were five minutes as we talked development. This was my passion.

At the airport, we parted with a handshake. He smiled at me and said, "Paul, you have great ambition. I know you are going to be a success at anything you put your mind to."

I watched his private plane taxi down the runway. My city was going to grow even more.

A week or two later, Sheldon's secretary called. He and Ed Shay, his partner on the power plants, from Pacific Engineers, wanted to invite Susan and me down to Los Angeles, ostensibly for us to check out their operations. I assumed to also confirm Sheldon's instincts that my city was the right one.

Edward Shay, who founded Pacific Architects and Engineers, was legendary in the industry. PAE was on its way to being a billion-dollar company and was a huge government contractor building massive projects for the U.S. government, as well as projects in Tokyo. (He owned whole blocks of Tokyo, in fact.)

For these two men, the city of Los Angeles was their oyster. Sheldon was a member of the very famous Hillcrest Country Club—where you could not even be considered for membership unless you gave away 10 percent of your earnings to philanthropic ventures each year (and you had to prove it!). It was the country club Hollywood heavyweights like Jack Warner, Samuel Goldwyn, and Louis B. Mayer were once members of. Because these legends were Jewish, decades ago, they could not be members of some other prominent country clubs in Los Angeles, thanks to unbridled bigotry. Thus, the Hillcrest Country Club was founded.

Dinner was delightful. Wine flowed. But it was at dinner that Sheldon said that I would, in fact, be more valuable to the Pollock Corporation if I came aboard to work *for* them rather than working *with* them in my capacity as a city manager. Sheldon had alternative cities he could easily transfer the project to, but I would be an asset to his company.

I had not expected that. I graciously said, "Sir, I'm honored. But I have every intention of making the leap to the private sector as an entrepreneur. Being the city manager is a stepping stone, and it got me out here to California and taught me still more things about development. But my destiny is to be self-employed and calling the shots—I've known it since I was a child. And that's what I'm going to do."

But Sheldon was never one to be deterred. "Yes. But believe me, it will be worth your while. We have bigger projects as we operate nationwide, and this is just one project of many."

He was very impressive—the kind of person who commands a room. But I had my own plans. "I appreciate it. But I'm going to walk my own path."

Susan and I returned to our hotel later that night. I've learned to be very decisive in life. I could not afford to feel a pang of regret for turning Sheldon down. I made the right decision for me. And Susan, my love, once again supported me.

The next morning, just Sheldon and I had a breakfast meeting. To my surprise, however, he did not want to finalize the details on building the power plant in my city. Instead, he looked across the table and told me, "I know what you said about wanting to be your own man. So, I have a proposition for you."

"OK," I said uncertainly.

"Your brains, my money."

I wasn't sure I was hearing him properly. "I beg your pardon, sir?"

"Your brains—my money. You form a company. You are the president of that company. We're going to give you a percentage of shares of the company. I am going to bring Ed Shay in, and we go three ways."

I am sure I hid my shock well, but after all, I had really just met the man twice before.

"Now," Sheldon added. "With all my money, you could run off to Hawaii and spend it all on a mistress. I can lose my money, but you can't afford to lose this opportunity."

However, I considered the obvious—this would be a huge conflict of interest.

"Sir, I would never want this to appear like a conflict of interest occurred."

"Neither would I. This is completely aboveboard—my offer has nothing to do with your city. It's about hiring *you.* And we'll make sure that's very, very clear."

Here I was, a city manager, and this man I had met only once before had decided I needed to be a part of his team—a *partner* on his team. I felt like a man who found a winning lottery ticket in the pocket of an old jacket in his closet. This was life-changing—so much so I almost didn't trust it. But that's another lesson—when opportunity comes, you'd better grab that tiger by the tail and hold on. Sheldon was an outside-the-box thinker—a person who taught me to think even bigger than myself.

I didn't need to think any more about it. I said "yes." Never one to burn bridges, I did as he instructed as far as making my city aware of what I had been offered by notifying the city attorney, mayor, and city council. I met with attorneys and waited for my contract from Sheldon and Edward. Attorneys drafted my letter to the city council—I turned over my oversight of the power plant to others, so it was completely hands-off and by the book. I also continued working for my city until they found a suitable replacement, and during that time, the city attorney and others handled the power plant without my involvement.

Then Sheldon, Edward, and I formed Tri-Coastal Development, where I was both president and principal shareholder. I had made a leap to both the private sector and entrepreneurship in a single huge move. Life was about to get extraordinarily interesting.

Does fate step into our lives? Luck? Determination? Grit? Self-belief? These all work together. But this life I was going to be entering happened because newspapers wrote about my "magic" with municipal bonds and transforming a sleepy, rural municipality into something more. Sheldon saw those stories and became curious about me. That's the role of fate. But the determination and self-belief—and ingenuity—propelled me to transform my city. Which came first? The chicken or the egg?

Sheldon let me make my own decisions—he expected me to take the reins, to lead, to let nothing hold me back. We set up an office in the city of Fresno, and I started creating divisions for Tri-Coastal. One of them was consulting services to municipalities. I would go to municipalities with the deep knowledge I had of city management, and I would do for other cities what I had once done for my own city. We would charge them consulting fees—because it was complicated work. But no one complained—because soon those municipalities were making lots of money and transforming their landscape just like my city had done.

One more thing on stretching toward big ideas. Early on in my time with him, I told Sheldon I was considering buying an anchor store in a shopping mall. He nodded and said it sounded good. "But," he added with a slight twinkle in his eyes, "why not buy the entire shopping mall?"

Here it was—the opportunity to tap into my biggest ideas meeting with the capital to do so. Life was changing at a rapid pace.

One addition to this story.

Years later, I found an identical flute to the one we sold to buy our first house. *And bought it for Susan.*

Reflection Questions

1. When has opportunity knocked for you? Did you boldly answer? If not, what do you think held you back?

2. How much do you cultivate outside-the-box thinking? How can you cultivate it more?

3. In today's climate of many things being done via text, email, calls, and Zoom, do you think there is still value in "face-to-face" in-person meetings?

4. How risk-tolerant are you?

5. What's the boldest idea you ever had? Did you act on it?

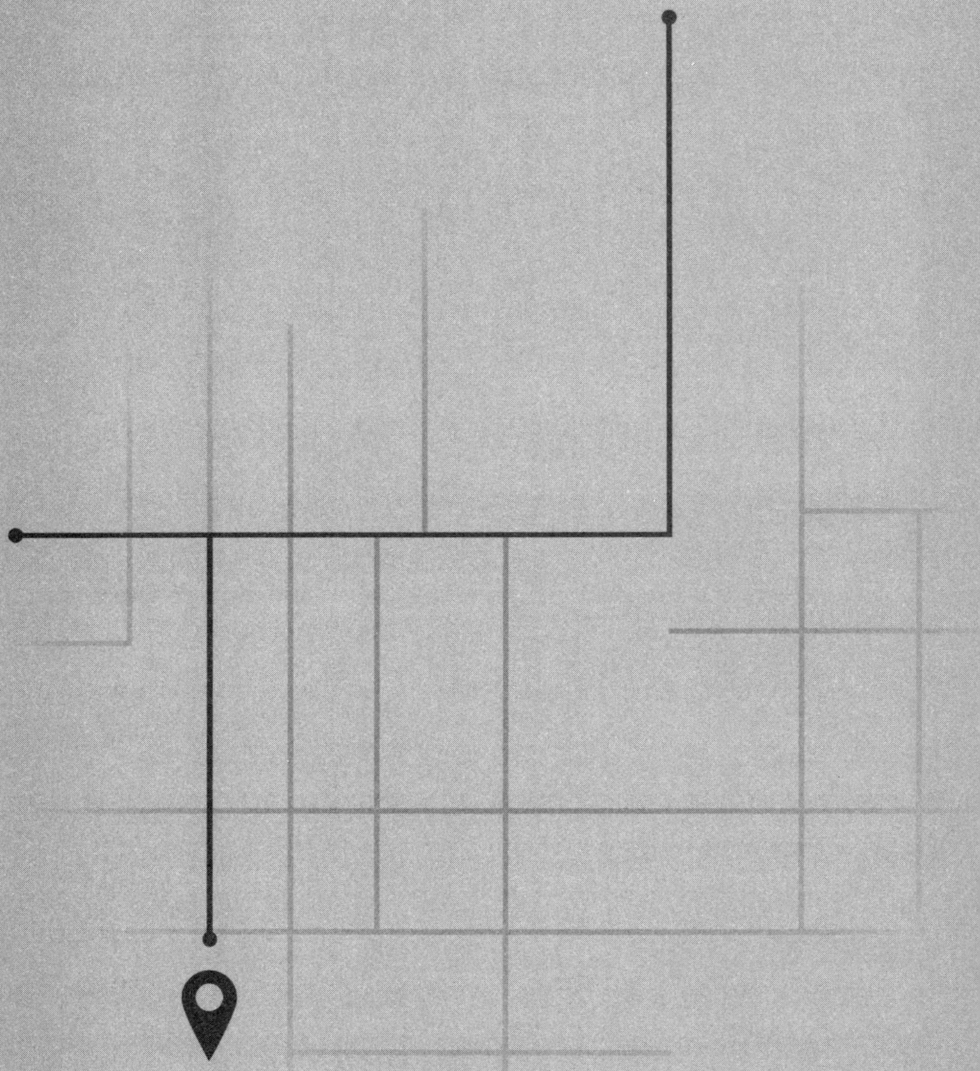

CHAPTER SEVEN

Playing in the Big Leagues

It always seems impossible until it's done.
—NELSON MANDELA

What followed were my high-flying years. There were times when I would place a "wake-up" call request from whatever hotel I was staying in, and I would be called at six o'clock the next morning and the first thing I'd ask was, "What city am I in?"

I was on a private plane at least three or four times a week. Sheldon was crisscrossing the country, too, as our companies built impressive hotels and high-rises, power plants, and more. We spent more time with each other than we did our families. We inspired each other, I think.

To create the kind of success we did, there are sacrifices to be made. Very often I was the voice on the telephone to my children instead of reading the bedtime story and being there with them. Were it not for Susan's ability to run our household and to be an amazing, involved mother, I am not sure if what I accomplished would have been possible. She enabled me to pursue success.

And I did.

One of my assets to Tri-Coastal, where I was now president, was my knowledge of the inner workings of the government. My background as city manager made me the ideal liaison with the local government for projects that we had. You know the saying, "You can't fight city hall"? You can if you know what you are doing.

We did millions and millions of dollars of business. Sheldon placed me in charge of all of the national development projects. I was in my early thirties and had a great deal of power to pursue projects I wanted. It was like being given the keys to the candy store. Whatever I could dream up for our company, I could pursue. There were no limits on my imagination—or my energy.

The beauty of the Sheldon Pollack Corporation was the total concept I discussed in chapter 6. We had in-house experts in all fields. In essence, any department needed for large real estate development deals. Then Ed Shay of Pacific Architects and Engineering rounded out our triumvirate, and they had all the in-house staff for construction of power plants/co-generation facilities. So, a combination of the Pollack Corporation, a national company, and Pacific Architects and Engineering, an international company, created a dynamic force. I basically was involved on the development side: execution of contracts, negotiations with the government, and others. As a team we were able to achieve what we were after—each had a role to play.

To give an idea of the types of projects—the level these were at—I have to tell the story of the late billionaire investor, Larry Tisch. Everyone knows him as the former chairman of CBS.

Larry Tisch was considering investing a hundred million dollars in a co-generation power plant we were building. Try to imagine—I had gone from improving a city in Central California, a center of agriculture, to flying on a private jet to negotiate with Larry Tisch.

On the flight there, Ed Shay leaned back in the Cessna's leather seat and remarked firmly, "If he doesn't give us this significant investment, we're just going to walk out." He pontificated on what he would say to Tisch if our demands were not met, growing louder and more animated, and a little worked up. When you work with powerful people, you are used to their bravado. We tried to soothe Ed. I assured him that everything would go smoothly. Our deal was a smart one for an investor, and I had every faith that Tisch would be on board.

Except that all didn't go smoothly—and it was Sheldon who salvaged the deal.

We landed in New York, where a stretch limo awaited to take us to Tisch's corporate offices. I had to smile to myself, remembering my arrival to New York City so unceremoniously over fifteen years prior. In those intervening years, my life had completely transformed. About a half hour later, Sheldon, Ed, and I were ushered into the inner sanctum of Mr. Tisch—an office designed to impress with a million-dollar skyline view to match.

We exchanged pleasantries, and then Sheldon began our pitch. Unfortunately, Ed, who was strongly intent on getting his way, was severely diabetic. While it was mostly controlled, diabetes can be unpredictable. And that day, of all days, he was having some sort of reaction, which caused him to nod off and be groggily out of it. Sheldon and I exchanged surreptitious glances, but we were doing fine covering for Ed. Larry Tisch heard us out and said we'd have his investment.

But we didn't pop the champagne cork just yet because suddenly, Ed roused, put up his finger, and affirmed, "We have plenty of other opportunities, so, if you don't meet our number, we will go elsewhere!"

The room went silent. But if you don't learn to think on your feet in business, you are doomed. Sheldon did just that. He laughed, "Ed is such a joker. *Thank you so much for giving us everything we've asked for, Mr. Tisch.* This was a very successful meeting, and we appreciate your time."

I stood, "Yes, we know what a busy man you are. We'll let you get on with your day."

Sheldon stood, shook hands with Tisch, and then placed a hand firmly on Ed's shoulder. "Let's go, Ed. Isn't it wonderful Mr. Tisch is going to give us the investment we want?"

Fortunately, Ed was picking up the clues, and we hustled him out of there and then took him out to eat as his sugar was low.

Sheldon was a marvel to watch in negotiations. He had the undeniable and undefinable "something" extra, charisma to spare, and was very shrewd and smart. We went from strength to strength, deal to deal. Here I was, able to tap into the expertise of both companies, both led by giants in their fields. Later on in my career, I was able to also work with John Q. Hammons' company. He was a legend in the hospitality arena. I was very fortunate, in partnership with John Q., to develop a multistory hotel in the Monterey Peninsula. This particular Embassy Suites is the tallest building with an ocean view located on Roberts Lake, and it is considered one of the most successful Embassy Suites in the country. By the time he passed away in 2013, he had built over two hundred hotels in forty states.

I had entered the big leagues. Not just the big leagues—the pinnacle of my chosen area of development. Very few people ever have the opportunity to enter into a career at that level. Not only that, but I was a kid as well. Sure, a little past thirty, but in the grand scheme of things, I was now jetting off to far-flung cities to sit across from household names negotiating deals at a very young age—soaking up the experience of giants.

At the same time, in my core, I was unchanged. I often say to succeed you must know yourself and be truthful with yourself and operate with integrity. There is a 1934 poem by Dale Wimbrow called "The Guy in the Glass." It's a poem most have read—often attributed to an anonymous poet. The poem is about a man looking in the mirror—and needing to be accountable to that man reflected there, above all others. Part of my confidence is I know the man in the glass very well.

Another lesson I hope to impart in this book is the power of studying and learning from the best. Anyone who thinks they know everything is sadly mistaken. I was surrounded by these billionaires who really knew their craft. And my goal was to watch them, to see how they do it. Why they got the deals they did, where they excelled, how they did it. I learned from all of them—mostly what to do and a couple of "what not to do" things. I was learning more than most would studying for an MBA.

In some ways, Sheldon was a father figure and a master teacher. He was my mentor—and we were both able to confide in each other. That two-way communication line enabled us to grow Tri-Coastal. I watched him think on his feet—and I got even better at that. I received a call from Sheldon one afternoon, telling me he was supposed to meet with someone very important about possibly investing with us, but he had been urgently called away. He told me the address and asked me to drive there and make apologies for him. I'll admit, I wasn't thrilled at this assignment, but off I went.

The address was for legendary Hollywood director Robert Wise, an Oscar winner for *The Sound of Music* and *West Side Story.* Of course, I showed up at his condo. But to be honest, I was too busy at that point to keep up with all the comings and goings of Hollywood. I had no idea who he was other than a "potential investor." (Had I known more, I would have been aware that his films championed racial equality and tolerance and that he was known for his work ethic.)

I drove to Santa Monica, and Mr. Wise lived in an incredible condo, the penthouse, contained behind gates and *several* layers of security. I had never seen such a striking building. Designed by the architectural genius I. M. Pei, it afforded magnificent views. I rang the doorbell, which sounded somewhat like a gong in a symphony. A maid answered, complete in a black uniform and apron. I explained who I was, and Mrs. Wise came to the door a short time later. She was an elegant woman with dark hair and dark eyes and a ready smile, dressed impeccably, with a jangling gold charm bracelet laden with charms on her wrist.

"Madam, I am so sorry, but Sheldon sends his regards and asked if I would come to talk with you and Mr. Wise instead. He's been urgently called away."

Never underestimate the manners taught by the Jesuit priests in my boarding school.

Mrs. Wise let me in and told me he wasn't home yet. I had never in my life seen a home like this. They had Picassos hanging on the walls. Monets. Each in a heavy frame and lit from above by carefully placed lighting and art sconces. It was gasp-inducing.

Mrs. Wise was charming and smiled and said, "Kid, do you want to tour this house?"

It was hard not to react as she took me room to room, pointing out the paintings, this sculpture or that. It was like being offered a tour in a private museum. I was awed by this collection.

Finally, we returned to a luxurious living room, their taste classic and sleek. She asked, "Kid, what are you drinking?"

I was so young—I liked wine and beer, but I had not acquired a taste for spirits. "Whatever you're having."

She spoke to a maid, who brought in two scotches a short time later. Mrs. Wise and I then sat, sipping our drinks and chatting. She was fascinating in her own right. Through Robert, she had been in rooms with the most powerful people in all of Hollywood. She was quick-witted—and told a good story, often punctuated with her throaty laugh. She had a bawdy sense of humor and was incredibly down to earth.

Eventually, Robert Wise came home—a handsome man with pale blond hair, very quiet and self-contained. I again explained Sheldon's circumstances, and he and his wife invited me for dinner, and we had a lovely evening, full of the grace of Old Hollywood. I actually never brought up the investment, because connecting person to person is so much more important. I was building a relationship—not for any "sales" purpose but because these were two interesting people.

When I left, Robert said to me, "Tell Sheldon it all worked out fine, and whatever he wants to do is a go from me."

Later I called Sheldon and delivered the good news. I was proud because I knew that had I not been able to hold my own in that situation, he would not have sent me. We were developing, day by day, deal by deal, even more trust.

Another lesson anyone who was around Sheldon and was observant would learn is to be "real." I think that's why people were so drawn to him—one of those charismatic people whose energy shifts the room in a positive way. (We are all capable to shifting the energy of a room—for positive or negative.) But with Sheldon, what you would see this of this man at a party was exactly what you would see at work, and you could see him at home that same way. When he walked into a party, he was bigger than life, and before long, he would be surrounded by people listening and laughing to his stories—a consummate storyteller. He loved people—he loved having fun, and he loved charging hard in business. He lived life truly to the fullest—and always as himself.

I realized then—and believe it now—that people respond to authenticity.

I responded to that authenticity. And our investors, and Sheldon and Ed themselves, responded to my business instincts.

We had vision—building the Hilton Hotel in Las Cruces, New Mexico, which had a lobby filled with light from arched windows, a terra-cotta roof, very much in the mission style for both the building and the décor. We were building condos and high-rises.

We also ventured into an area I had expertise in: bonds and revitalization projects. We went into the affordable housing market—which the state of California and the government incentivized through tax exemptions. For Tri-Coastal's first project in that arena, I created three hundred units—the Annadale Terrace Apartments—with the grant that I received, which at that time was the largest Housing Urban Action grant ever awarded in the state.

By being "total concept," I had the freedom to pivot. I might close one deal for low-income housing. Another deal might clean up and redevelop a blighted area. Next, I could utilize the commercial division to create a beautiful hotel—hotels that are still standing. Plus, as I covered previously, we had a consulting side that helped other cities develop utilizing my same methodology.

I also saw that Sheldon's company was its own little city. What I mean by that is if you took all the people who worked for us, all the people the contractors used when they built our projects, all their partners and spouses and children and family members, we were responsible—through our success or our failure—for many other lives. I share this because it is far too easy in books to share success after success and make it all sound as if everything turned to gold. I was aware of the pressures of success—of knowing so many people relied on us, and now all these years later, on me.

I truly believe you must be diversified. Diversification allows you to go with the ups and downs of the seas of business. Put all your efforts in one place, and it might be like the *Titanic* when hard times come—it all sinks. But with diversification, one sector could be stronger than another at different junctures in time. Diversification lets me sleep at night. My involvement and decisions have balance since I cannot afford to let anybody down.

Maybe the pressures helped me hone my instincts. I know my own success in decision-making comes down to several factors, but two in particular are your craft and your instincts.

I had gone to graduate school, I had run several cities, I had formed redevelopment agencies—I had earned my education, if you will, in my chosen path. I arrived well-versed in the craft. In my business, I needed to be an expert in that craft. So often, we think that only the writers and the artists of the world are the "creatives." But if you are a true entrepreneur, you will be creative as well. Your timing needs to be precise. Your knowledge needs to be very detailed. You must sit across a table, face to face, discussing companies being bought and sold for billions. Then you, knowing your craft, sit back and determine if that company or deal is worth the price. If you are not ready yet, then study from the best—but get that education.

Next was my instinct—my gut. You must be your own man, woman, person. You have to develop in business in such a way that you know you can trust and listen to that intuitive feeling you have about a deal—good or bad.

That same instinct is important because to be as successful as possible, you also have to take the pulse of the local community and the people who will be most affected by your projects. Remember my story of the stolen trees? I made a mistake by coming in like gangbusters without developing trust and local investment in my plans first. Once I involved people, things turned around completely.

Sheldon and Ed were very happy with my work. So much so that Ed Shay took me to dinner and tried to hire me away to work just with him. He pressed his case over a very expensive dinner at a steakhouse—the kind with steaks that are two inches thick and so perfectly seasoned that you can practically cut them with a butter knife. Ed was eying me for a large role in his company. I liked Ed very much, and I thanked him. But I did have a deeper rapport with Sheldon. I personally liked Sheldon, too, but we also spent so much time together, days and days—on planes, in meetings, at lunches, at dinners, in limousines on the way to the airport. We had a stronger relationship.

The next day, Sheldon and I were having lunch at Hillcrest, when I told him straight out about the conversation I had with Ed. Remember that I have always felt you must face the man in the mirror. I did not want any hint of deceit between us. To be frank, I think Ed was just a competitive person, not trying to do something to screw Sheldon. To people like that, everything is part of the exciting game they play, always looking for an edge. In any case, Sheldon upped Ed's deal and offered me still more incentive and freedom to pursue work with him. In the end, Sheldon and I bought Ed out, and Sheldon and I continued our winning streak.

Meanwhile, another important aspect of my success is that, despite, by this point, working with famous people and billionaires, meeting producers and movie stars, businesspeople at the highest echelon, my head was never turned. Part of my head never being turned was my values. I am someone who makes connections. Those could be in business. Friendships. With people across the world while on a trip into the Amazon or in a village in Italy or in an inn in Patagonia. I connect with the janitor or the bartender as much as I do the CEO. This is another reason I sleep well at night. I've been the immigrant with a few hundred bucks in his pocket. I've been the car wash guy. I know how to survive without screwing the other guy.

I also had a confidence that was born of an unusual life—being self-sufficient at age four! I don't know about you, but if one of my children or grandchildren came to me, beat up, nose bloodied, I would not send them off to deal with it themselves. But we cannot choose our childhood circumstances. For me, they drove me to success.

Another success principle I learned in my life, and further learned in my time as the president of Tri-Coastal, is that you do not accept "no" for an answer. But let me tell you what I mean by that. You can be told no and then no again. The potential client can tell you—definitively—that they do not want to do business with you. At some point, a no is a no (for now). But the way I view it is a no means "work harder." Let's say you got a no because you don't have enough experience in a certain area; then you increase your knowledge and skill until you demonstrate you are, in fact, worthy for the project.

With the Pollack Corporation and Tri-Coastal, we did not hear no that often. Sheldon used to end each day by sticking his head in my office and grinning and saying, "Did we make any money today?" And what he meant was not really, "Did we make any cash today?" He meant, "Was today productive?"

Sometimes I would say, "Not really Sheldon"—because we all have those days. Ever Mr. Personality, he would wink, or his eyes would shine as if he was in on an inside joke, and say, "Me neither."

We both loved the thrills of the chase and the challenge of it all. Sheldon owned a plane—he was a very experienced pilot. This let us fly the Cessna from city to city, meeting to meeting, wherever we needed to be, wherever opportunity was. I never had the bug to become a pilot myself, but I would sit in the copilot seat next to Sheldon as he flew us high above the clouds. It is truly a different experience to be in the cockpit instead of in the back of a larger passenger plane. There is a certain freedom in the skies, looking out on the vastness both above and below you.

We had offices in Fresno and Santa Monica among other cities and business all over the United States. We were working on a project on the California coast on the Monterey Peninsula. I was meeting with the mayor of a town called Seaside for a multistory hotel and neighborhood shopping center.

I called home that afternoon, and Susan greeted my call sounding a little weary.

"What's wrong?"

"It's nothing, really. It's just that Michelle misses you very much. She's inconsolable. She's been crying." (I can tell you, as a father all my children had me wrapped around their pinkies—and here my little angel was crying.)

She was ten years old, an age when they really do miss their parents. (When they are thirteen, sometimes they pretend they don't know you! Let's not even get into when they are in high school.) She wanted her "Papa" to take her to her favorite pizza place. I glanced at my watch. I could work this out. Trust me, you get used to juggling all those balls as a parent and a businessman. "Tell her I will be home in time to take her out for pizza."

Sometimes I traveled with Sheldon—and sometimes I took my own transportation as it wasn't unusual for us to be headed in opposite directions for our next meetings. However, this time, with Michelle upset, I told Sheldon, "Listen, can you drop me off at the Fresno airport? I'll spend the night at home." His next meeting was in Las Cruces, New Mexico. I said, "If you need me, just call, and I will catch a flight in the morning to Las Cruces. Otherwise, I will see you in Los Angeles."

We flew in from Monterey in the Cessna as the evening sky turned from pink to gray-blue. I remember a few stars hung in the sky, looking like I could grab them. It was moments like that when Sheldon and I would be silent for a moment, sharing a spectacular view.

Sheldon had thirty-five years of experience as a pilot—I trusted him to land us safely every time. We taxied down the runway, he dropped me off, and we said our usual goodbyes. I told him I would see him in either Las Cruces or Los Angeles.

Like many a busy working parent, I was delighted at this stolen window of time to be with my daughter. I drove home, picked up Michelle, and listened to her happily chatter to me in the car, and I took her to the pizza joint. I sat across from her and gave her my undivided attention.

The next morning, pre-dawn, very early, our house phone rang. It was Sheldon's daughter, Eileen. "Do you know where Sheldon is?"

"He ended up dropping me off in Fresno, and he went on to Las Cruces."

"Paul … the plane never arrived."

I am not sure how long it was before my heart beat again. But then I did what most people in my situation would do. I rationalized a hundred reasons why Sheldon had not turned up. Everything from got tired and decided to stay in a hotel to hoping, almost, that he was having an affair and off somewhere. Anything but the chill that was spreading up my spine.

It turned out that Sheldon took off again after he dropped me in Fresno, and then he crashed in the Arizona desert. Why was inconclusive. Perhaps the cabin depressurized. He was an exceptional pilot—perhaps he had a heart attack.

What I did know is that it felt as if the earth opened and I fell into a chasm.

In that horrible, tragic moment, in those days surrounding it, I lost my best friend. Sheldon's family and all who knew, loved, and treasured him—and even negotiated fiercely with him—lost an amazing man.

I lost my mentor.

And shortly after, I lost everything that I worked for.

Reflection Questions

1. Name a time you thought "on your feet" in business. What did you learn from that experience?

2. How often do you feel you display your "authentic self"? What (if anything) is the difference between your business persona and your personal one?

3. What are you doing to diversify your business so that you can ride any highs and lows in your business sector or your investments?

4. Name a time you didn't trust your gut that you regret.

5. Have you ever had a moment in life where you lost it all? How did you recover or what are you doing to recover?

CHAPTER EIGHT

Starting Over

New beginnings are often disguised as painful endings.

—LAO TZU

Grief is a strange beast. It haunts and hunts us, insidious and painful. For months, I wrestled with my own deep pain over losing a man who was like a father to me, a mentor, and my business partner while trying to offer solace to all the other people missing this remarkable man as well. He left behind a wife as well as six children and a complex business with many moving parts.

Most of us, in grief, are the walking wounded. I think of it as a dreamlike state. We're part of the world, but we're also deeply distracted. We're struggling to find our emotional footing again. In my case, I also had to find my business footing again. It would not prove easy.

In those months, I learned how important it is to have a succession plan or legacy plan. Sheldon was in wonderful health, had the sharpest of minds, had the most charming of personalities, and was too young to have fully contemplated what would happen if he passed away. Any plans of that sort were no doubt, in his mind, years and years down the road.

Unfortunately, my assets were tied up in the company, both Tri-Coastal and my position within the Pollack Corporation in development projects. His family had very tough decisions to make and were forced to make drastic changes to the corporate structure, including reevaluating ongoing projects nationwide. So, though it was personally damaging to my own fortunes, I understood. We were *all* numb and doing the best we could.

Remember, too, that Pollack was a "total concept," as I have mentioned a few times. The problem with that was it had a massive payroll. (I now tend to hire consultants and external firms to avoid too big an in-house team.)

Sheldon had *personally* guaranteed several notes (something I never do—and learned this the hard way from watching what unfolded). The notes were coming due—and banks and investors, while sympathetic, have businesses to run. Sympathy goes but so far. The notes needed to be paid. In the end, I truly had lost it all.

Except, of course, the most important assets of all—my family and my own drive and passion. I had long before learned that Susan would have stood beside me if I were making pizzas in the local pizza parlor or had millions. But I was faced with the prospect of being broke—it was staring me in the face—with no partner and no means to move forward as Sheldon and I once had.

At the time, Susan and I and our family lived in beautiful Calabasas, California, which is about twenty minutes from Malibu. Our house was on the golf course, with picturesque views. I went home after a particularly brutal day as the company was dismantling.

The end was near. Susan was sitting outside by the pool. The sun was near the horizon and getting ready to set.

"You look upset," she said softly to me.

I felt more than upset. I was unsure of my next move. "I'm concerned."

For the most part, Susan and I compartmentalized a bit—at least I did. When I was home, I tried to be a father and a husband and pour my affection into my family. Susan and I had our own wonderful conversations—we both liked to travel, we both had our interests, and we, of course, were parents and talked about the kids incessantly. I shielded her from my business situation. But now I needed to explain it all so that she could understand the precarious position we found ourselves in.

"Susan, we're on our own. My money—our money—was intertwined with Sheldon's business."

As a developer, you don't tend to keep a lot of cash on hand—you are sinking your assets into the next big project, the next land investment. You put a lot into it and then get a huge rate of return (if you know what you are doing—and have a little luck).

Susan said, "OK. I understand. How much money *do* we have?"

"We have our house. And we have a $100,000 line of credit against it."

She looked at me then with her blue eyes and asked, "All right. Then what are we going to do?"

I assured her I would figure it out and not to worry. As a testament of what an extraordinary woman I have had by my side, she made plans to earn her master's and then doctorate in audiology so that she could work and bring money in while I did, indeed, "figure it out." She did this as a full-time mother and a woman involved with charities and so much more. Over and over again, our partnership has survived.

I can tell you, when I look back on my own story, I can see the role of *relationships* and *friendships*. And this period of my life was no different. Or perhaps I am merely a cat with nine lives.

I took a cold, hard look at my circumstances. I had a wife, three children, a life they and I loved. We had a beautiful home. The children went to wonderful schools. But I also had mortgage payments and expenses. And no obvious way to recover from this setback—except I had my intelligence, my entrepreneurial spirit—and solid relationships with people who trusted me. *That* was my best asset at this time.

I had a friend named Jack Riley. I phoned him and explained my situation—I was very frank. Obviously, in our sphere of development, people knew about the tragedy of Sheldon.

Jack explained that he had a friend with a piece of property back in Central California in Fresno County. There was a tax-exempt bond against the property for several million. The property was zoned for apartments or residential. Through my connection with Jack, he thought I could pick up the property for a small sum.

I immediately drove there and met the young man who owned the property—he was in his early twenties, drove a beautiful Porsche, and was very wealthy. A bright guy, pleasant, but he had inherited the property from his father—and he did not understand tax-exempt bond financing.

I did, but I didn't have the full purchase price. This put us at a crossroads. I explained this to the young man who owned the property but told him I would figure it out. Here I was, after many years of hard work and having essentially unlimited assets at my disposal, having to piece together my financing.

I will cover in chapter 11 that without the people who make this ride of life important and special, what the point would be. Susan and I are fortunate enough to have some wonderful couple friends. These are people we go on vacations with, go skiing with, and are part of one another's lives. Our ski partners happened to be mostly doctors, and they lived in Fresno. I had dinner with them a couple of nights later. I laid out the situation, and I told them I was going to try to formulate a plan to somehow leverage my line of credit on my house to purchase this land. I told them this story with no artifice—no agenda other than sharing my current situation. To my shock, they said, "We're going to be your partners. Let's buy the property together."

Moments like that, when people convey to you their trust, are those that stick with you forever. I raised the funds from my dear friends, bought the land, hired an architect, and designed the houses the way I wanted to build.

Now, at that time, in that area of Central California, the homes offered were cookie cutter, bland, and without any exceptional details. They offered no luxuries or special concepts. I was determined to change that.

Once again, friendships and relationships were going to be my salvation. I went to my local bank in a three-piece suit. I sat with the president of the bank who happened to be recommended to me. I asked, again with my firm belief that honesty is the best policy, "Do you want the good news or the bad news first?"

He smiled at me across his desk and folded his hands. "All right, Paul, give me the good news first."

"The good news is I have been a city manager for multiple cities and municipalities for years. I know what I am doing. I've acted as a developer of one of the largest companies in California, overseeing nationwide development." I rattled off all of my credentials, the projects I had done with Sheldon, Ed Shay, John Q., the sheer scale, and the types of investors we had.

"That's the good news." I leaned back in my faux-leather chair opposite him. "The bad news is that my partner's plane crashed. All of my own money is tied up in the fallout of this tragedy. I have no control over this. I was a shareholder in Tri-Coastal. I was the key principal of our development company. And right now, I might as well be encased in cement as far as my cashflow."

The banker nodded. "I remember reading about the crash. I'm very sorry, Paul. That is a really tough turn of events. And I know you were close."

"Thank you." Every time I brought up Sheldon, still, I felt a pang in my chest. "So, to climb out of this mess, I bought a large piece of residentially zoned property with a much higher value than what I paid."

He was curious how I was able to acquire the property for a fraction of the value. So, I explained the concept of Mello-Roos financing, a popular method in California for the installation of on- and off-site improvements via the issuance of tax-exempt bonds. He was familiar with the concept.

Now, I'm going to tell you a little aside. I did have a plan for a residential development. Because a young, barely twentysomething man who was the son of a friend wanted to learn the business and had approached me. Even after I explained my situation, he was ready to sign on with me to learn everything he could about real estate development. He also had extraordinary computer skills. With his help, we were able to create a prospectus, beautiful plans, and presentations of what this development could be. It may have been him and me on a dining room table and a basic office I later rented, but the presentation was as professional as if we had been a billion-dollar company.

I slid my folder across the table. "I would like a loan for the cost to build two model homes on the property."

The banker asked how much I needed, and I told him the amount. He didn't blink. And I walked out of that bank with a guarantee of a loan for that amount.

Next, we built the model homes. For that area of the state, the development was an oasis. A gated community, the houses embraced light; they had higher-end finishes, and this is what young families aspired to. The development embodied my vision. Fresno County was used to tract housing. Sameness. However, I had seen homes in Calabasas and other areas that had small lots (obviously land in most areas of California is very expensive), but they paid attention to details. The houses were often two-story with high ceilings, big windows, and so on. I thus reproduced what I liked and what I had noticed people desired. At the time, in Central California, they were not accustomed to this. The news traveled quickly about the development. In addition, I did semi-custom homes. If a buyer wanted to pay for me to knock down a wall, or to make a change to the layout of the bedrooms, I would, as long as they were making these decisions up front.

It was not long before the development was sold out. I made several million in twelve months.

I was on my way again.

Only this time, I was very much on my own—this was mine and mine alone. After my experiences, this was the way I knew it had to be.

I bought my doctor-friends out, so appreciative for the risk they took in me. They got handsomely compensated, and everybody was paid. And I took the money I made, and I used it as seed money and evolved to the next project and the next. The projects got bigger and bigger, all the way from 1990 with a hundred thousand negative cash flow—because it was the bank's money. It wasn't my money. And now I was again surfing in the big waves.

One example is in the early 2000s, when the University of California built a campus in Merced, California. It was their tenth campus and the first new one to open in decades. It was also the first research university built in the entire United States in the twenty-first century. I went ahead and bought five hundred acres contiguous to the university. I knew that a college is more than simply a campus. A university location of that size will need a surrounding community to support it. Where would the staff live? The students? Where would the children of professors go to school? Where would everyone shop? I spotted a huge opportunity.

I master-planned a five-hundred-acre community consisting of three thousand homes, roughly six thousand apartments, a police station, churches, and a bus depot, creating a small village. This has always been one of my favorite parts of what I do. When I can see a community, a development, a vision for a waterfront, a hotel, whatever it is, rise from nothing, and I know it was me who was involved in its creation.

Meanwhile, the University of California was spending *billions* right next to where my newly planned community and five hundred acres was. Soon, I had an all-cash, forty-eight-hour close from a company out of Utah. They flew down, and they fell in love with the project, with my vision.

I said yes on the spot. I am always playing the long game. So, for example, you may recall when I took the job in Fresno County, California, originally, it was to get me relocated to the West Coast. Now, I happily agreed to the deal because my long game was *not* to be developing in Central California. I wanted to get back to the coast. That the offer was all cash made the deal even better.

I now had that much more money to create deals and destiny.

I even did one deal for a dollar.

Yes, $1.

There was a very large shopping plaza with a major grocery chain that had once been its anchor. But now the grocery store had gone out of business, and the entire place was empty and an eyesore. No one wants a situation like this in their community. Empty locations like that attract trouble—and crime.

I called the corporate headquarters of the grocery store, and I said that I'd buy this project from them and take it off their hands. They told me the price. I said, "Fine." I did not negotiate at all. But I put down a single dollar in escrow for an option to buy it. Then I flipped the property for millions of dollars. I made several million—on a dollar investment.

I don't want to give the impression that I brushed off the death of my mentor and went on, "business as usual." I like to think, wherever he is, he is proud I landed on my feet. I found myself building on strength after strength. Much of what I did, I had learned in my time with him.

Then one day, I heard from my friend, Jack Riley. Of course, Jack was the one who had arranged for me to buy the property in Fresno to start over—and for that I would forever be grateful.

He was full of warm congratulations. "Paul, you know, your success is amazing. Everybody's talking about your development and everything else you are doing. Considering what you went through, it's a heck of a turnaround, my friend."

"Thanks, Jack. You helped set it all in motion."

"Well, I have something for you that I think you will find intriguing."

My interest was piqued. "Sure, what?"

"Have you ever done affordable multifamily housing?"

I really had not, but I was certainly open to it.

"Want to do a few?"

I said sure. I had some concept of it—but to be honest, not at the scale we would end up pursuing. Jack Riley understood the process, but Jack did not have the funding to take on the scale of these projects. While I was now more than in the black, I also couldn't fund a massive multifamily housing project.

We then, the two of us, went to Los Angeles to meet with the chairman of SunAmerica and then AIG. These are two massive insurance companies. SunAmerica's chairman was Eli Broad. Not only was he named among the top one hundred richest people in the United States, he was an incredible benefactor to the arts. Instead, we ended up meeting with the president of SunAmerica Housing, Mike Fowler, and his executive vice president, Doug Bigley.

Both SunAmerica and AIG (and later other companies) had made a groundbreaking decision to embark on a new concept at their insurance companies.

As Eli Broad said at the time in an interview, "We're going to build multifamily affordable housing. We need the tax credits to offset our income from the insurance company. But we're also helping the community."

They wanted to do this as a tax shelter. They were thus looking for people like me to come in and be the managing partner. The deal was they put up the money and I went and built the project—the vision, the know-how, the building expertise. They got the tax credit, and my company got to own the apartments at the end of the project.

We ended up building, acquiring, and renovating thousands of apartments under that program with SunAmerica insurance company as our limited partner; the same with AIG. We would then transform those apartments into affordable housing. Eventually, Prudential and others came calling. Before I really could comprehend the amazing opportunities that were coming my way, we were in partnership with multiple Fortune 500 companies, doing the building/developing—which was my passion. We were the general partner of all these projects, so we ran the development, they provided the financial backing, and soon we had a portfolio of an amazing number of units that were lovely places for people in need of affordable housing. It is honestly hard to understand that if you are not from an area like New York City or most of California, where housing prices push most middle-class and working-class people out of the market. We all deserve a place to call *home*.

Ostensibly, my partners in these ventures were the insurance companies and also Jack Riley. But after a bit, I began to chafe at the idea of partners. So, I bought them all out. Again, I think after the trauma of losing Sheldon, I saw that I did not want others second-guessing me. I wanted the simplicity of being on my own.

As I sit here today, our company owns or has owned thousands of apartments, all the way from Hawaii to Texas to California to Nevada, all different places—and always expanding. We rent apartments to young families—and we rent to students in college towns.

Very few people make their fortune once.

Fewer still make their fortunes twice.

Even fewer than that do so as a first-generation American who arrived with less than $500 in his pocket.

You know, it has been over thirty years that Sheldon has been gone. So much has transpired. But I still can't help but feel sometimes as if I had an angel on my shoulder.

I still sometimes measure decisions by, What would Sheldon have done if he were still here? How would he handle this?

Sheldon Pollack had taught me not to have limits. From that first time when I told him I was going to buy a store in a shopping mall and he told me to consider buying the *entire* shopping plaza, instead of just the store, limitless thinking has been a part of my world.

I learned two important things during this time in my life.

First, I learned that what I carry with me—my business acumen, my integrity, my smarts and ingenuity, my love for family and friends—are the only things I need to make my way in this world.

The second thing I learned is there is no such thing as not coming back from the brink.

If you made your fortune once, look at it this way: you know how to—so you can do it twice.

Reflection Questions

1. Who are the people you totally trust? How have they supported you in business or your personal life?

2. Business setbacks can be devastating, but it's important to learn from them. I learned lessons about personal guarantees, about succession plans, and more, in the face of tragedy. What is a lesson you learned the hard way, and how have you ensured you do not make that same mistake?

3. In the aftermath of the stock market crash of 1929, people who lost it all jumped out of windows rather than face the loss of everything. Had I not found my worth in other things—in my family, in my own talents—I might have had a very different outcome. Maybe I would not have had the courage or energy to start over. What is your *value*? It is more than things.

4. Have you ever reinvented yourself and had an Act II?

5. What do you think your legacy is?

CHAPTER NINE

The Concentration of Success

There will come a time when you believe everything is finished; that will be the beginning.

—LOUIS L'AMOUR

We all love the underdog, don't we? Some of the greatest movies are those focused on the little guy who hit it big, the walk-on football player who makes the team, the person who was counted out but who had one more big score or triumph up their sleeve. These stories are thrilling because we all want to believe we have another act in the play of our life. I am dating myself a little, but long before people were watching movies on streaming services from the comfort of their living rooms, and they were packing into movie theaters, I can remember people literally cheering aloud in the movie *Rocky.*

It is a strange thing, too, starting over. Sheldon's death had been utterly devastating. However, like a fighter staggered by a knockdown blow, I struggled to my feet again to finish the round and start a new one. When you start over, there's a brutal double edge of freedom. You are completely aware of the painful reason you are starting over. But when you have nothing left to lose, it provides you with the daring and courage to reach for new heights of success.

As usual, whatever you want to call it—kismet, a dash of luck, fate—I was placed in the path of people who enriched my life or who provided me with adventures both serious and silly. Success without friends and family is meaningless, but I will save that for chapter 11.

I was also able to construct my company in a way that served me well—from the lessons I had learned from my mentor, both the mistakes he made and the successes he soared to. I will present my success formula later in this chapter along with some of the essential elements to embody if you want to aim high.

Concentrations of Success

When I walk through the citrus groves of my farm in Ojai, I am surrounded by the intoxicating scent of lemons, earth, and perhaps fresh rain. My Malibu house projects onto the beach over a rocky crag. When you are in my living room, you feel as if you are on the deck of a ship. But if I open the glass doors and step out back and I take in the beach, up and down its beautiful shore, all paths lead to successful people. I can literally point to houses (some of which I have built) of NBA stars or movie stars, or men and women achieving unprecedented success in their chosen fields—this is even more intoxicating than the scent of lemon trees.

I've given it some thought. Some people speak about energy vortices—places like Sedona that believers think have extraordinary metaphysical energies. I don't know if that is true or not. But I do know that there are some places on the earth—New York City, London, San Francisco, Hong Kong, Los Angeles, Dubai, Seoul, Tokyo, Sydney, and my Ojai and Malibu—cities and locations that seem to draw thinkers and creators, people with big dreams and ideas. Then, if you are lucky, if you put out your own creativity and energy, your own passion and hunger for success, you ultimately cross paths with gifted people who will have a positive impact on your life and your career.

If I would have arrived in the United States and taken other detours, settled at any other place, I might not be where I am. I live and work in places with sky's-the-limit potential. I live and work and develop properties in places with what I call a *concentration of success.* Who would have believed the boy carrying his grandfather's sack in Iran would end up in an epicenter of successful people and exciting potential?

But in my heart, I still never forgot where I started from. It is impossible for me to read news accounts of some of the events and changes that have occurred in Iran and not know my journey has been blessed by good fortune. The air on the beach I enjoy so much is imbued with the winds of freedom—and I never forget it. I breathe free because I came here decades ago as an immigrant. But I am aware that freedom is not free. *Freedom* flows through all I do.

Occasionally, I have looked around the room or across the boardroom table and smirked to myself. No one else is in on the joke—but inside I know. How is it that my life has had so many twists and turns? Over the years, in Hollywood, Los Angeles, and Malibu, I have had many surreal experiences. For example, I attended the Emmys with our dear friends, Mike and Liz Young. They are producers who won multiple Emmy awards—and as I clutched one of the golden awards after they won (those statuettes are heavy, by the way!), I managed to playfully fool the BBC journalist attending and conduct an interview in which I pretended *I* had won it.

I've interacted with European royalty, with journalistic royalty. For example, I encountered the late, great Barbara Walters. As is often the case when I meet someone who is a legend, I merely wanted to express my admiration to her for her contributions to journalism. After I shook her hand, I told her in a very innocent way that by having the privilege of shaking her hand, it seems I am shaking the hand of all of the most famous people on the earth. She replied very humbly, "I never thought of it that way." She could not have been more gracious.

I've worked with and met sports stars and movie legends. As a boy, I loved race cars and idolized Steve McQueen. I would skip school and go to see his movies—he projected a "cool" image that all my young friends and I wanted to emulate. I also avidly tried to see every movie of Dustin Hoffman, whose acting I admired. Years later, I became dear friends with Steve McQueen's son, Chad. Dustin Hoffman is a neighbor. And I bought another acting legend's home—Anthony Hopkins's serene paradise in Ojai (a place whose serenity is so important to me to this day). At times, the concept of "pinching" myself comes to mind. Dreams and idols of a boy from far across the world ended up being reality. Who does all this happen to?

Not only that, but I think in a place attracting great actors, actresses, creatives and writers, and so on, there is a palpable energy. And you also run across memorable eccentrics. One of my favorite lighthearted stories was when I worked on a project in the city of Pacifica, near San Francisco, right on the beach. The vice mayor, John, called and said he wanted to have lunch with me in Los Angeles because he was on a business trip. I picked him up in Santa Monica. We were going to an Italian restaurant, and he said, "Do you mind pulling there around the corner? I want to meet up with my brother. I just want to say hi."

Sure enough, a short kid—in his twenties—stood on the corner with his hands in his pockets. He had huge, sort of "bug" eyes, and before I knew it, he had hopped into the back of my sports car. Grinning, he said, "I'll go wherever you guys go."

Shrugging, I drove on to the Italian restaurant, and the vice mayor's brother, Rob, entertained us both in the car and at the restaurant. He was hilarious—able to riff and make sarcastic comments about any topic.

Over the meal, I asked Rob what he did for a living.

"I'm a comedian, and one day I will be on *Saturday Night Live* and you'll be watching me. I'm also gonna do movies, and you're gonna watch all of my movies. And my name is Rob Schneider. Don't forget—don't you ever forget." And then he paused for a moment and said, "I bet you want to know who my favorite comedian is."

I had never met anyone quite like him. "Well, no, but if you want to tell me …"

He pulled a cassette tape out of his back pocket. (Yes, I am dating myself.) He handed it to me and said, "This comedian, Emo Phillips, is my favorite. Here. This is my gift to you for being so kind."

Well, there I was a couple of years later, and who should be on the television on *Saturday Night Live*, but the eccentric young brother of the vice mayor. He was right. I would one day be watching him on the television.

As much as that surreal story makes me (and I hope you) smile, I tell it more for the sheer idea that I had been born clear across the globe. To think that one day, I would be in Los Angeles, meeting people from every industry, including show business, demonstrates that you simply never know where your path will lead, the people you will meet, the accidents of happenstance and serendipity that will place you in one situation or another. I have even been named

California Businessman of the Year. My journey has been filled with struggles—and peaks, with hard work and recognition, with adventure and excitement. Isn't that the delight of life, sometimes? We never know what is around the next corner, where our next project might come from, and what person we know who will connect us to someone else and that will have an impact on our life. Consequently, I have always viewed the winds of fate, both good and bad, as part of the journey. I have delighted in meeting all sorts of people on my path of life—and I have accepted that hard times befall us all. The ups and downs, the silly and the mundane, the heights of success, the moments of courage, and the moments of doubt, as well as the pains of loss affect us all.

Even my house is an accident of good fortune. Susan has always wanted to live on the ocean. One day the Realtor I was working with called me and said, "I have the most unusual house in Malibu. It is falling apart. But there is nothing like it because you are extended into the ocean and people go under that house as they walk the beach—that's how far it projects into the sea."

I flew down to Malibu, and the house was everything she said it would be. A beautiful piece of property that seemed part of the ocean itself—and a wreck of a house. It belonged to the bank, and the man who owned this house was from a religious denomination where he had taken multiple wives. On top of this, he defrauded the banks with fake appraisals and borrowed money against those inflated properties.

The bank wanted an all-cash, as-is escrow in twenty-four to forty-eight hours. This was the *only* time in my life I did not negotiate. I will even bargain over pizza! At the last minute, the attorney representing the lender wanted a very large fee over and above the cost of the home and the closing. I told my Realtor, "Done!" I think my Realtor thought I had finally lost it.

But I knew what this house could be. I tore down the structure and built my forever home with Susan—in a place with a concentration of success.

In fact, I was so impressed with the location of my house, I ended up purchasing the house next door with the thought to demolish and rebuild the home for investment purposes. Among others, the home was previously owned by Ted Danson. I happened to be at the Ojai Inn and Spa at a later date and recognized Ted Danson as we both sat in the lounge area, and I told him I bought his beach house in Malibu. He was surprised and, in a funny way, asked what happened to his bedroom. He told me many entertaining stories of his time in the home while sandwiched between Steve McQueen and Keith Moon, the drummer for The Who. I found Ted Danson to be a great storyteller, and we could have continued the conversation for several hours were it not for the scheduled spa services each of us had. I also learned that the house was originally built by Mr. Walt Disney for his daughter, Diane. Apparently, I demolished a beach house with an amazing and long history!

My Success Formula

In the meantime, my company was flourishing, and we grew on strength after strength. I had very specific ideas about how I wanted to do things, including not being overleveraged and, unlike Sheldon, not having everything in house. This makes my company sleeker and nimbler, and that's how I like it.

When I started over after Sheldon's death, my company could be anything. But over time, my business instincts have honed it down to a system, diversifying in ways that protect me and my company and its people. Under the umbrella of Pacific Rim Companies, there are multiple entities specializing in the following areas:

Affordable Multifamily Housing: I think affordable housing is an important issue facing the country—all families should have a safe, clean, nice place to live. In places like California, housing can be exorbitant, but it is a struggle everywhere. We own several thousand units in Nevada, California, Hawaii, and elsewhere. Affordable housing developments restrict occupancy to lower-income tenants, determined at a percentage of Area Median Income, and rent is capped, annually. We sometimes develop affordable housing projects along with very large companies, Fortune 1000 companies included. However, some are my own independent projects.

Market Rate Multifamily Housing: The market rate division provides housing for people without special needs for reduced-cost housing. This could be a typical subdivision or community. I try to truly have a vision for what people want, on the pulse of beautiful design.

Student Housing: The difference between student housing and standard multifamily housing is that student housing usually has proximity to a university. For example, as some colleges have grown, they have not been able to dedicate enough budget or land for new dormitories. Allowing developers like me to come create beautiful student housing is a win-win for all.

From a personal standpoint, I am a father and a grandfather. I would want my kids to live some place that is well built. From a financial standpoint, student housing means you have a captive audience that you can rely on at least nine to ten months out of the year. We own several thousand units of student housing in California and Texas.

At Texas A&M, we have one project that sits on thirty-eight acres of land. In order for you to get from one end to the other end, you have to drive. That secretly thrills me—it's another legacy. We own multiple blocks within less than a mile from the university. Again, it is really gratifying to realize you have an impact on a community—that you are responsible for the housing of thousands of people who rely on you.

In the case of student housing, market rate housing, or our affordable housing division, we hire the very best management companies to run them. I certainly don't want to get a call at midnight that a pipe is clogged. However, I want to make sure that the needs of the tenants are attended to promptly and professionally and that the assets are well maintained.

Between these three divisions, we provide housing for tens of thousands of people—couples, families, seniors, students, and singles, across the entire board as far as income is concerned. It is like my company is a small city taken as a whole—which is a very satisfying feeling. When I consider how many people have housing because of Pacific Rim, I feel as if I am leaving a legacy.

Single-Family Semi-Custom and Custom Homes: My company has built single-family subdivisions ranging from luxury to very luxury. These are magnificent houses with unique designs and all the bells and whistles. I myself love "smart homes," so these are outfitted with the absolute latest and greatest tech that lets the owner run the house with the touch of a button.

Commercial: The commercial division specializes in the development of various commercial projects ranging from neighborhood to major anchor shopping centers.

Construction: Two of the companies under the umbrella of Pacific Rim Companies are licensed general contracting firms based in California and are involved in construction of multifamily housing and renovation of existing apartment complexes. The companies operate solely for the benefit of our wholly owned projects throughout the country.

Mental Health Services: California Psychological Institute (CPI) provides professional mental health services to children, adolescents, and their families. The staff consists of licensed mental health professionals and registered interns. In addition, CPI offers bachelor-level Client Care Coordinators, who provide rehabilitation, education, and in-home services.

CPI provides services for youths throughout Fresno County and the Central Valley. CPI serves youths of all ages, including infants, children, teenagers, and some young adults. CPI conveniently offers a full range of mental health services under one roof, including therapy, infant mental health services, medication services, psychological testing, and court-ordered bonding and sibling assessments.

My daughter, Michelle, has served as the chief executive officer of the company for over twenty years. It is so important to be surrounded by people you can trust—so much is on the line. My daughter, Jennifer, is my chief financial officer (and brilliant in the role)—she controls the money side of our operations. Keely is the one who knows what I know—all the plates that are spinning at one time. If I am unavailable, she is the one who can speak to people on the particulars of our projects. She is on the development side. She joined my company in her twenties and has learned the business beside me.

In addition to all of these, we also acquire and reposition assets. Because of my head for numbers, and my outside-the-box thinking, repositioning is something that I'm very good at. I'll buy a large multifamily property that needs help or restoration or significant rebuilding in a good neighborhood, and I will make all of the changes and repairs. This allows us to enhance the neighborhood, raise the rent a bit, and increase the value of the asset.

How do I spin all those plates?

First, every morning when I come into the office, I have an assortment of reports waiting for me, with highlights of what needs my attention. To keep it all straight, I actually tackle it by *region.*

I also firmly believe in decentralization. If I needed to be worried about every single asset that we own, I would have an ulcer. Our company engages national management companies, the largest in America, that handle the day-to-day operation of our assets. They run it; they take care of it. I watched Sheldon keep everything in house—and that is also a fine way to operate. But it also involves tremendous overhead. Decentralization alleviates much of that.

Next, I have construction managers who are smart and intelligent. I would rather earn a little less profit and pay people a little more in order to attract the best. This is especially true when we are developing projects far from our home base. I certainly do not want to be hopping on a plane to put out proverbial fires. I want my construction managers to handle things, deal with the contractors, and ensure the project is going smoothly.

Honestly, because of my unique background as a city manager, I think state and federal governments should consider decentralizing instead of holding tight to everything. If they decentralize and pass certain elements of infrastructure creation and other areas of governance on to experts in the private sector and *hold them accountable* (and I know that's a big if), believe me, you and I will pay less taxes.

I am also very cautious not to offer personal guarantees. I have seen too many of my peers and colleagues ruined or certainly put through very difficult financial stresses by signing personal guarantees. Those guarantees are made with the idea that everything will go smoothly. Too often, that "worst-case scenario" comes to pass. I do not mind paying a higher premium to get what I need in the form of a loan rather than having a cheaper loan with personal guarantees.

When you live through the unthinkable (e.g., a business partner perishing in a crash), you want the security of guardrails. God forbid, if the market crashes and you own, let's say, a hotel with a $50 million recourse loan, you are held personally liable for the entire debt, versus a non-recourse loan that would be limited to the asset without further liability to the borrowing entity.

When I consider the concentration of success around my company and the people in it, I think of a few things. I have watched each of my three children, now adults, make their way to their own success. My daughters, Michelle and Jennifer, and my son, Christopher, are successful because they started from the bottom, from zero. When they came aboard my company as young people, they did everything that nobody else wanted to do. They swept the floors and answered phone calls. They grew in their roles—and Christopher eventually went off and formed his own company that, among other projects, designs and builds luxury beach estates for the elite of the elite, the household names. These are stunning homes, and he concentrates in major beachfront cities in California, operating from Malibu. Christopher holds a degree in architecture from the San Diego School of Architecture, and he is a licensed contractor and real estate developer operating in multiple states. I am so pleased to witness his success based on his hard work and experience. Jennifer, as I stated earlier, is an integral part of Pacific Rim as the acting chief financial officer and is heavily involved with the multifamily and student housing projects nationwide. Jennifer holds two bachelor's degrees in business finance and psychology from the University of Colorado at Boulder. Michelle serves as the executive director of California Psychological Institute, a wholly owned subsidiary of our company. Under Michelle's leadership,

California Psychological Institute has expanded to become one of the largest mental health service providers in Central California. Michelle has a master's degree in public health and a bachelor's degree in health science, both from California State University, Fresno. Success means being willing to put in your dues.

I will be honest—living where I do, where money flows freely, I have seen people hand their children everything. This is almost always a recipe for disaster, and I have witnessed many ruined lives. Success comes from *putting in the work.*

Next, each individual in a successful operation has to contribute to the team, but the person who's the head of that team, who is at the helm, needs to know enough about all aspects of the business to be effective. I look to see where the weakest link in my organization is, and I concentrate on that with laser focus. It takes hours and hours and hours to find a solution to make sure that the weak link disappears.

Success is a contact sport.

By that, I mean success has to be created on the ground. It must be woven into the fabric of your company. There can be no passing the buck. A lot of people have my cell phone number, including tenants. Now, if I get calls, I expect my management company to handle the issues, but I demand a written response to the tenant to make sure that the individual is taken care of. When you do that, people begin to understand that you care. You also have to give them a good product.

While I'm troubleshooting, I also keep an eye open for any new opportunities that could be attractive to the company or any of the divisions of my company. Another avenue to success—always be alert for opportunity.

In addition, I spend a great deal of time, along with my daughter, Jennifer (our chief financial officer), meeting and interacting with various lenders throughout the country. As your career moves forward, if you have real estate development ambitions, it is not how much money you make but how you finance it. On major projects, let's say worth close to a hundred million dollars, a half a percentage point can amount to millions. Therefore, your "concentration of success" must include lenders—it's very important to have a very close relationship with them. They must respect your reputation, they must trust you, they must believe you show a solid history, and then, of course, there is the credit that you have.

Here's the thing; by now, you must realize that my word is my bond. Remember my story about the man in the mirror. Once your reputation is tattered by cutting corners, or by not being a person of your word, or not caring about that person renting a unit in your building, it will take you a very long time—if ever—to repair it.

My next success principle is to *feel the pulse*.

The pulse is the pulse of the entire company and more. You must be acutely aware of what is going on at all times. At the levels of success I operate at, I have seen more than one person brought down by their losing touch with the pulse of their company and the people in it. The moment I see somewhere with a high fever, I want to know what the problem is.

Success depends on *you*. You need to always be "on" and aware of all the moving parts. Once you start to lose the vision of the big picture, you're in trouble!

Reflection Questions

1. Look around you. What is the "concentration of success"? What people, mentors, or environments can you reach out to in order to be around people who are going in the same direction as you are?

2. Success is a contact sport. What does that mean to you?

3. Every company or person needs to have a success formula that works for them. What is yours?

4. How does diversification impact your industry/niche/company?

5. How important is ensuring the next generation is not handed everything?

CHAPTER TEN

Take Courage

Fighting Back and Moving Forward in Gratitude

Fire is the test of gold; adversity, of strong men.

—MARTHA GRAHAM

Sometimes the trappings of success can mean people perceive you as having it easy. After all, you live in a nice home, or you have this achievement or that. But success does not mean anyone has it "easy." That could not be further from the truth. As your success grows, so does the size of your professional problems. Negotiating a hundred-million-dollar deal is most of the time a lot more complicated than a much smaller deal. More is riding on the line. I know if I have a failure of some sort, it impacts the people I am employing at my properties, or who are constructing buildings for me, the people who are planning to move into the communities I am building, or the community itself if I am building a shopping plaza or a hotel. The weight of responsibility bears down harder.

In addition, success doesn't inoculate you from unfortunate events or loss. I fought my own internal battle to come back from Sheldon's death, and I was once again reaching new heights. I was completely my own boss, which was pure freedom. I didn't mind the pressures of running multiple companies and divisions. I thrived on the challenges. I was in my element.

When I look back on my various jobs, I always dove in with maximum enthusiasm. That didn't matter if I was a captain at a catering hall—or negotiating to build a luxury hotel. However, I was to face new challenges that required me to dig deep once again and find within myself, and with the support of friends and family, the will and courage to press forward.

In 2011, the construction division team was renovating a beach home in Malibu. One of the elements of luxury homes I build and renovate is the tech; they are always cutting-edge smart homes. A smart home allows the owner to operate all sorts of systems from heating and air conditioning and Bluetooth to other electronic devices remotely through a phone app or computer. For example, I enter my home with my thumbprint—biometrics. I can press a button and doors or windows open, shades are lifted to view the sunny day, or lights are turned on as darkness falls. There is, of course, the best security, as well as the ability to control the temperature of various rooms or turn things off and on remotely, from far away. These days, these added tech goodies are something people increasingly want, along with "green" construction and luxury finishes. In addition to that, the homes I renovate or build are wired for sound/Bluetooth throughout. I can wander from upstairs to downstairs and whatever music is playing follows.

During the renovation of a house in Malibu, the last thing that needed to be completed was a speaker wire to be threaded and pulled from under a subfloor. The speaker wire was not connected to anything from either side. A young employee was to pull the wire with the understanding that a professional technician will connect the speakers for a sophisticated sound system. Unfortunately, by accident, the employee spliced a high-voltage wire, and he was electrocuted and died instantly.

First, of course, this was agony for his family. For the crew. For anyone who loved him. He was a young man, and he left for work that day and then did not return. What a horrific tragedy. The people who witnessed it were traumatized and, no doubt, went into a state of shock.

This was also one of the most devastating events of my life. Sometimes, when we go through tragedy (such as I had with Sheldon), we can fool ourselves into thinking, "Well, I used up my quota of tragic events … things should be good from here on out."

This is obviously not true.

I was devastated. In fact, when I got the call that this happened, I had to grip the counter to keep from falling—the room literally spun around me. Susan was equally distraught. My children were also just wrecked by this event. None of us had gone through something like this in all my years in the world of real estate development.

The employee's family sued one of our companies that he was employed by. I fully expected them to receive a settlement—I wanted them cared for. He had a wife. He had a child. This was a very unfortunate accident. Months of litigation followed.

I could not sleep through this whole time. Night after night, I was consumed with thoughts of this young man dying. I would toss and turn and then get up and wander around my house like a ghost. I was also, like any family man and business owner, fearful of losing all I had worked so hard to attain and to provide for my own wife and family.

During this time, I was difficult to be around—distracted, short-tempered, gloomy. I gained over thirty pounds—which made me feel even worse. I knew a young man was not returning home to his family, that his parents had lost a son, that his wife had lost her husband, and that a little girl would now grow up fatherless. However, I also wanted what was fair. Worse, as the case moved forward and we proceeded to court, I spent months in a courtroom looking at the members of the jury who seemed to already view me with hostility. I saw it in how they glanced at me, occasionally even staring me down.

I was a guy from Malibu, with a three-piece suit sitting in the courtroom. I think they saw me as a rich man who did not care—when nothing could be further from the truth. If only they knew! This didn't just upset me, but it upset my entire family as well. However, the opposing attorneys' job was to try to make me out to be the worst human alive.

If you look at the Bureau of Labor Statistics or OSHA, construction is one of the most dangerous professions out there—along with being a lumberjack, a derrick operator, a crane operator, and many other jobs with high accident rates, often from human error. One death is too many. But even the safest sites have mistakes.

From day one, as I said, I wanted a settlement. He left behind a little girl. The insurance company's lawyers, though, are paid to save the insurance company money. They kept insisting that the employee's choices that day amounted to a mistake and that the family had no case. I didn't care if they had a case or not! Settle! A man was dead.

However, then the other side tried to pierce the corporate veil. In the end (and I cannot write much more because of confidentiality agreements), the insurance company did settle. But it was months and months and months taken from my life, time in which I was so distraught that it impacted my own family and my relationship with them. It was a level of stress worse than when Sheldon died—and that is saying something.

I have learned that tragic events like these can be like the pull of a rip current. When I look out at the white-capped ocean, I know there are rips, currents, and dangers under the waves—but that, equally, riding the waves can be exhilarating. You cannot let yourself get pulled under.

However, after long periods of stress, there is always the need to regroup, to think about what you have been through, and to try to make sense of it. I was numb for a while, and even once the case was settled, it took me a while to move on, to be able to sleep again, and to reconcile the horrible events.

This trying time was not my only challenge in recent years. Three different hospitalizations were extremely serious: diverticulitis, a TIA, and then an operation that did not go according to plan. In one case, Susan and my adult children called a priest because it was quite uncertain as to whether I would make it.

It is at moments like that when you must determine what life is all about. I will save my adoration and appreciation for the people who have crossed my paths over the years, and the friends and family in my life, for the last chapter. But this entire book is a testament to the sheer will it takes to create success in business, to take on the drive and longing for freedom and ideas and vision, and to discern what it all means.

When I went through my TIA, I was in intensive care for two weeks, and there were moments, like anyone, I wondered, "Is this it? Have I lost the drive? Should I slow down?" But the answer I always heard, echoing in my mind, was no. I am made for what I do, and it feels—especially as I write this book and look back on all the events—like development was always my destiny.

One of the secrets of finding a pathway through all the difficult times has been meditation. I cannot advocate for it enough. Years ago, I read a book by Jose Silva called *The Silva Mind Control Method.* This book was life-changing for me. No, it does not mean I meet people and control their minds. It means I have learned to control my *own.* And that, I promise you, is power.

Regardless of how busy you are in life, if you do not learn to meditate, and learn to carve out moments to be able to allow your soul to leave your body, to travel to a meditative state, success will be that much harder for you to achieve. Our mind is like the compass that points to success and happiness if we only learn to control it and not let it control us.

I live in a place where there are celebrities and wealthy people—more than a few of whom are spoiled. No matter where you live or what you do for a living, you no doubt see it too. It's interesting (and sometimes a little amusing) seeing people lose it, people who have little control over their own emotions and behavior.

The Silva method is a holistic system of meditation and mind control training courses (as well as books) that helps you unlock your full human potential by changing your mindset. Used by people like Wayne Dyer and CEOs like Robert Stiller (CEO of Green Mountain Coffee and a *Forbes* Entrepreneur of the Year) and countless others, the methodology allows you to tap into your creativity and intuition, as well as to access the power of your mind, with its limitless potential.

Now, in a memoir, it is so important to be truthful, and I will confess, I used to have a short temper. If someone cut in front of me on the highway when I was younger, I would get so mad and I would want to chase the other car and driver.

The Silva method taught me what a waste of energy that is. I honestly believe if everyone could learn these meditation techniques, the world would be a far better place. Think of my example of chasing the car. Imagine if you had total control over your short fuse. If you ignore the road rage when someone cuts you off on the highway, and you pretend that didn't happen, in thirty seconds, you don't even know which car cut you off. That is how inconsequential it is.

In addition, it is not *reality*. By that I mean, suppose you assume that driver is just a hateful, obnoxious person. Your mind sort of runs off to the races—"How infuriating that person is!" However, the driver could be preoccupied. (Haven't we all made a dumb move on the highway without realizing it, like almost moving over a lane but then seeing the car in our blind spot and veering back?) Maybe the driver is racing home because of an emergency. Maybe they just got terrible news. Yet, here you have imbued that encounter with an anger or rage that simply is not reality—it's not part of the actual equation. *You've* added that rage.

So with the methodology, I learned to bring my anger from a nine, say, on a scale of one to ten, and bring it down, nine, eight, seven, six, and boom, it's gone. Like magic. Only you are the magician. Again, that is power. Now imagine harnessing that when trying to make a sale, or negotiating a contract, or determining the next course of action. Imagine harnessing intuition and learning to truly listen to what it is telling you.

I tend to break it down like this now when I face a difficulty: Is this a problem that will impact me five years from now? (Usually not.) What about five months? Five weeks? Five days? Sometimes it is not even five minutes! I even teach this to my grandchildren—because what a gift it is to learn these meditative techniques as a young person.

I wish I had been given the tools years ago. Far too many of us waste unnecessary energy on the five-minute problems in life.

Once you learn these techniques, they become second nature. It has changed how I engage with and move through the world. I think of it almost like a chess game. Instead of just moving pawns, and seeing a couple of moves ahead, I now can see the entire board and visualize twenty-five moves ahead.

Here's another example.

Many of us go into social situations, and before we are even introduced, we may form an opinion about someone else across the room. Maybe the person seems standoffish. Or maybe we think they must have a huge ego because of how they look or dress. Maybe we walk into a dinner party and think someone else looks angry. Once again, *you* are imbuing that person or situation with an emotion. However, how many times in your life have you discovered the standoffish person is actually painfully shy? Or that the person who looks angry is actually recovering from a death in their family? Whatever it is, what we *projected* onto that person was not reality. (And even if it is, this should not cause you to waste time contemplating it.)

I approach each person I meet with an openness of "let's see what this person offers." We can learn something from every single person who crosses our path (something I will discuss more in the next chapter). Now, let's say the encounter does turn out to be negative. Maybe this person is small-minded or deeply negative. Using my meditation techniques, I can turn even that around and think, "Well, I have gratitude and appreciation that I don't view life like that."

Another huge influence on my life is the mystic and poet Rumi. This thirteenth-century scholar was a seeker of love and human kindness. Never has his teachings been more important, perhaps, than the turbulent times of today.

I felt I needed to share the valleys as well as the peaks in this book. If you plan to pursue success, then you need to know at times you will face challenges that will require courage. However, that courage is inside each of us. It is in the darkest of times that we learn what we are made of. Then we get to take that knowledge with us as we face the next challenge as well as the good times.

Reflection Questions

1. What is something very difficult that you have overcome—and what teachable moments did you discover when you came out the other side?

2. What are your go-to techniques when you encounter frustration or anger in yourself?

3. In what situations do you find yourself projecting characteristics or emotions onto others? How can you handle that differently?

4. What are the five things you feel very grateful for?

5. Think of three problems currently weighing on your mind. Now categorize each one. Is it a five-year problem? Five months? Five days? Or five minutes?

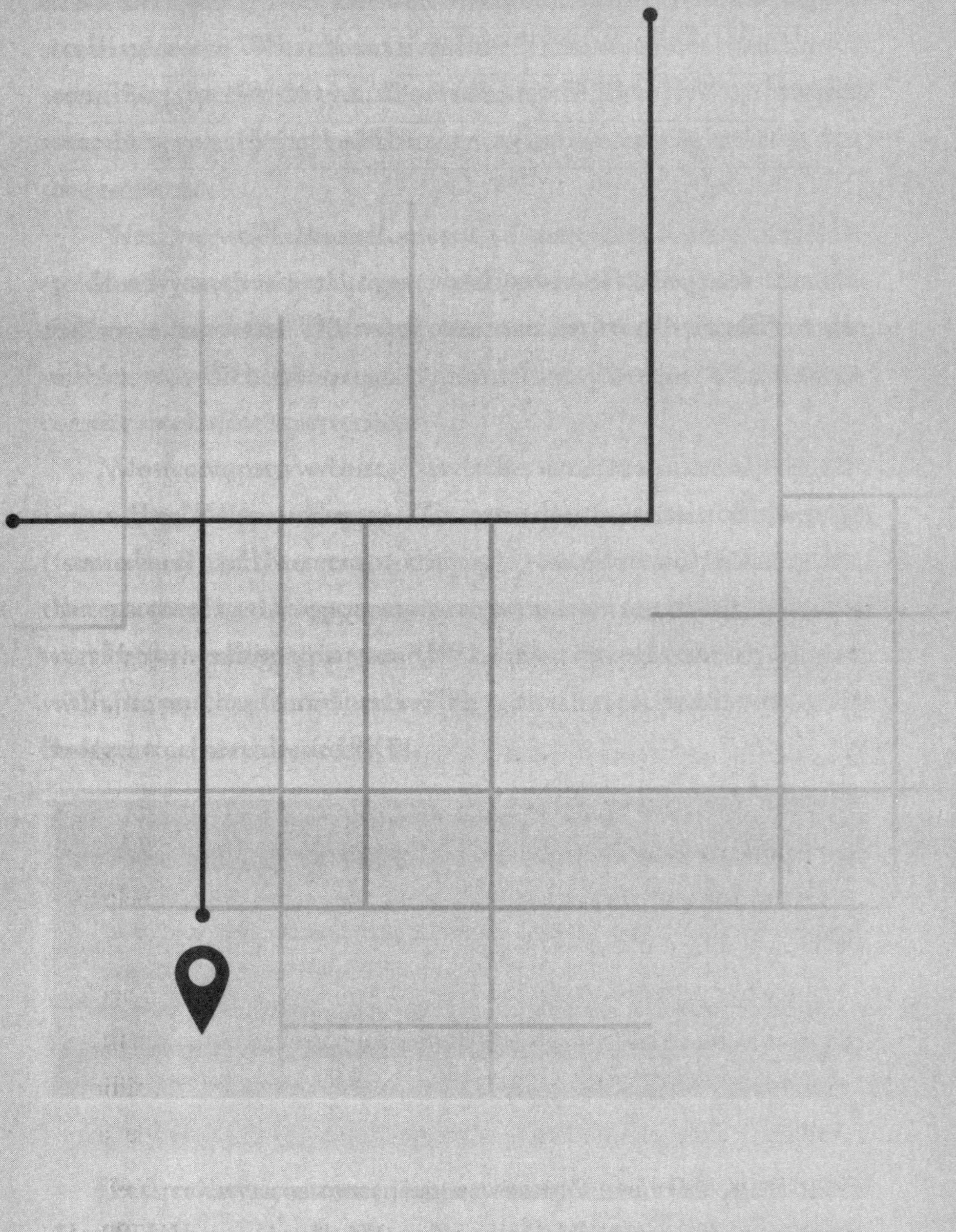

CHAPTER ELEVEN

Full Circle

The Meaning of It All

Set your life on fire. Seek those who fan your flames.

—RUMI

I often think of the blank date in the book my father gifted me when I left Iran for England. I knew I would not return. For someone else, the blank space might have felt ominous. But for a young man with an entrepreneur's soul and a love of freedom, that blank spot represented possibility.

I could create my own destiny.

Not the destiny my father had in mind for me or even my beloved grandfather. But my own, uniquely mine.

Since my departure from the place of my birth, I have traveled to most of the countries in the world. I have dined in some of the finest restaurants on earth. I have made deals worth hundreds of millions of dollars. I have planned cities. I have interacted with movie stars and sports legends, as well as captains of industry. I watched as my company erected magnificent hotels and extraordinary luxury homes.

I experienced the joys of witnessing dolphins joyously leaping through the waves in Hawaii and the sun rising over the African savannah, of standing on a glacier in Alaska and encountering indigenous tribe members in the dark depths of the Amazon.

But at the end of the day, absolutely nothing would be meaningful without my family and friends. In fact, I always think it is a huge tragedy when successful people do not understand that. My life would truly be empty without Susan and my children (and now grandchildren). They imbue my life with meaning. They are the reason I work so hard, and they have given me purpose and perspective.

But, like many people who chase their dreams of success, sacrifices were part of my journey. I was not the only one making sacrifices—which included missed events at home, good-nights and I-love-yous said to my children over long-distance phone calls, and not there, as I often wished, while reading a bedtime story. My wife and family were just as much a part of those sacrifices. If Susan had not been my true partner, I would have only achieved a fraction of my successes.

In addition, Susan and I were very fortunate—we ended up having deep friendships with a group of couples, all of us raising young kids at the time. This same crew of people are those we vacationed with, skiied with, celebrated holidays with, and supported one another through the good times and the difficult ones. Some of those same people were the ones who rallied around me when Sheldon died, enabling me to start over.

I am also lucky to have my path cross with my loyal and intelligent executive assistant, Keely, currently the vice president of construction and development of my company. When I met her, she was working in a bookstore and had no experience in the world of development and construction. I think, in some ways, we have grown together. Now, I watch her capably steering the ship, so to speak. I rely on her in so many ways—not only now as a project manager but also as someone within my organization who can read my mind a bit. She anticipates what is needed next—and having a true "right-hand" person means I get to focus on what I do best—creating deals.

It is the people who have made my life so interesting and worthwhile.

One reason I enjoy traveling so much is the opportunity to make connections with others who might live thousands of miles away from me and have totally different life experiences. Yet, we can explore our common humanity. This makes our wide world a little smaller, a little more human, a little more about peace and caring.

For example, Susan and I along with a group of friends cosponsor a school and schoolchildren in Africa. We have visited them—an uplifting and treasured experience. Africa is an extraordinary place—in some places it is tropical and green, whereas in others the sun beats down relentlessly on the harshness of a desert. In still other places, savannah grasses offer a home for all kinds of exotic animals from elephants to lions, from rhinos to ostriches.

When we arrived at the school, I was struck by how little, in terms of material possessions, these kids and their teachers have. The buildings are very simple, with the supplies not enough to go around all the time. The children were all dressed neatly, but I know most only have a couple of uniforms, and they try to keep them clean and wear them with pride. The African continent has been ravaged by AIDS. Some of these children are without parents. The world has been cruel to them already—except that is such a misconception.

While Susan and I arrived with books as gifts, I fully understood we were the ones receiving the gift.

It is so easy, in our modern world, with every convenience, to take it all for granted. These children have so little, yet they radiated joy.

They sang for us—pure voices of innocence. At lunchtime, they were all more than happy to share with us. They had great affection for their devoted teachers—and they played with one another without bullying or exclusion. Perhaps the people of Africa have a secret to life that we cannot understand despite all our first-world advantages. I have tried to take this concept of gratitude in all circumstances home with me.

Aside from my family and friends, perhaps what I am most grateful for is more of a concept than something tangible. *Freedom.*

Every day, across the world, men of deep principles and courage are persecuted for ideas and ideals. After the fall of the Shah in Iran, I appreciated in an even deeper way what my journey has meant. When there was a regime change, what family I had left in Iran lost everything. Their citrus trees were deprived of water as the water rights were seized and the trees all withered and died.

Of all the many places I have visited, two caused me to have moments of deep grief and clarity and appreciation in that regard. Susan and I traveled to Vietnam as well as, on another trip, to South Africa. In Vietnam, we toured the infamous "Hanoi Hilton." This was the brutal prison where the late senator John McCain and many others spent years being tortured, brutalized, and starved, with untreated illnesses, infections, and injuries during the Vietnam War.

While much of the original camp was knocked down in the 1990s, there is still a museum—a reminder of human's inhumanity to human and a desire for peace. Sadly, it seems we never learn these lessons as a global society.

When I visited McCain's cell, I touched the walls, and I *felt* the terrible energy that permeated such a hallowed place. I think when any of us visit such grounds, we wonder, *Would I have had such courage in the face of exhaustive, relentless pain?* I am grateful every day that

I emigrated to America before I ever had to face such a question in real life.

The other place I visited that evoked such deep emotions of gratitude and harrowing sadness was Nelson Mandela's prison. His cell on Robben Island was no more than eight feet by seven feet, and he slept on a straw mat on a cement floor. To give context, this was not "way back when" in the 1940s and 1950s (or earlier). Nelson Mandela was not freed until 1990.

Think about that. In 1990, I was already making my way through my career in the United States. I had a wife and children. I had *freedom.*

Visiting his cell, for me, considering how deeply I admired Nelson Mandela, was almost like a religious experience. On the tour, no one spoke; in the hush, we all considered what this great man had experienced—the same view, day after day, the harsh sun and brutal heat, separated from his family. Yet not hopeless.

I could not help but glance at Susan and clasp her hand. Then I walked to the wall and pressed my forehead against its rough surface. How had he not fallen into deep despair? Both he and John McCain somehow found strength from within, from their God, from knowing that their cause and beliefs were just.

With that blank space for my return to Iran, I could appreciate their sufferings and admire their commitment to humanity.

In 2022, I lost two very dear friends unexpectedly from my core group of close friends. It was heartbreaking because they were friends of decades. There is no life unscathed by loss or tragedy. By the time you are older, you will have mourned friends and family; I lost my father during the COVID pandemic, for example. By a certain age, you—or your friends—will have endured the peaks and valleys of life. It is rare these days to have a core group you can truly rely on. We're a busy society, and I sometimes even wonder if those tech devices we all love so much are ruining the way we make and keep friends. These are those "two a.m." friends—the ones you know if there was an emergency, they would answer that call in the middle of the night and show up with whatever you need. Their losses affected me deeply.

From the birth of my first child right up to today, my children have been one of my prime motivators. It doesn't matter that they are all adults with careers and lives—they are still my kids and always will be. I feel incredibly blessed that I was able—in this improbable life of mine—to have been able to provide good education, unconditional love and support, experiences of travel, to give them what I didn't always have.

Maybe it was the boarding school—sleeping on a bed in a roomful of boys, our only "entertainment" being a bedtime story read by one of the priests—that made me doubly certain I wanted them to have a deep knowledge of how treasured they are. I am grateful my son worked with me at the beginning of his career and that both my daughters are part of my businesses in one way or another.

And finally, how could I have done any of this without Susan? Here we were two crazy-in-love kids—both of us still in school!—deciding to commit to each other for life. I do not have to tell you that it doesn't always work out for couples. Yet here we are, still best friends, still going off on our adventures, still creating the best life we can for our kids and grandkids. With the right partner by your side, it is like a secret weapon.

And now here I am, tens of thousands of words and many stories of business, determination, and plenty of luck and smarts later, reflecting on all these lessons I carry with me.

I live with no regrets. I live with the love of family and friends. I live with my successes and adventures. I live with the scars of losses that we all must bear. I live with a love for wanting to leave a legacy and the world a little better than how I found it.

And most of all, I live with that man in the mirror.

From a faraway place, I arrived at the corner of Destiny and Ingenuity—Determination and Love. I arrived, after journeying many miles and years, *home*.

Reflection Questions

1. Who are the people who make your work and life meaningful? Have you told them lately?

2. What are the legacies you hope to create and leave for the next generation?

3. What does freedom mean to you?

4. What are the "street corners" of your life? Destiny and Fate? Love and Determination? What do your signs read?

5. Can you name an encounter in the world that demonstrated to you it's a smaller place than we may think at times?

____

____

____

____